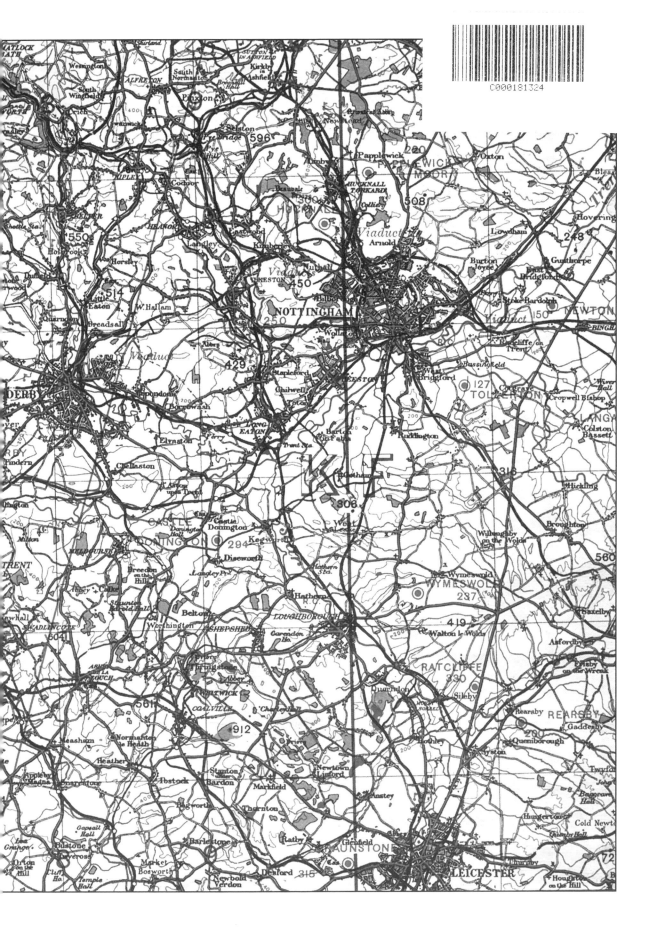

The RIVER TRENT

The schooner G.R. Berg *under tow at Morton Corner, heading downriver after unloading her cargo at Gainsborough.*

The
RIVER TRENT

Richard Stone

Phillimore

2005

Published by
PHILLIMORE & CO. LTD
Shopwyke Manor Barn, Chichester, West Sussex, England

ISBN 1 86077 356 7

Printed and bound in Great Britain by
CAMBRIDGE PRINTING

For Thomas

Contents

List of Illustrations

Frontispiece: The schooner *G.R. Berg* under tow at Morton Corner

Acknowledgements

My thanks to Carol Allison, Rodney Coldron, Jeff Clifton (Shardlow Heritage Centre), Sid Brumhead, Ruth Needham (OnTrent Initiative), George Wilkinson, Alan Gifford, Alan Kimber, Rev. John Quarrell, Nicholas Alfrey (Department of Art History, University of Nottingham) and to all the many individuals and organisations who have been helpful in the course of my research.

I am grateful for assistance from the staff at Millgate Museum, Newark, Bromley House Library, and at Local Studies Libraries and at the County Record Offices in Derbyshire, Leicestershire, Lincolnshire, Nottinghamshire and Staffordshire.

Illustrations: frontispiece, 7, 16, 47, 48, 49, 50, 51, 52, 136, 137, and, 145 are from the Local Studies Collection, Lincoln Central Library by courtesy of Lincolnshire County Council, Education and Cultural Services Directorate. Illustration 8 is reproduced courtesy of Bromley House Library.

Images: 42, 44, and 126 are from the Millgate Museum collection and are reproduced by permission of Newark and Sherwood District Council.

The map of Newark is reproduced from the 1900 Ordnance Survey map. End papers are reproduced from the 1943 (2nd War Revision) Ordnance Survey map (Air Sheet 6). Other maps have been compiled from various topographical surveys published by the Ordnance Survey between 1824 and 1880. In some instances, two or more sheets with different publication dates have been stitched and overlaid in order to produce an extract to match the arrangement of the text.

Author photograph by Karen Lanchester.

Special thanks to Helen Stone for drawings.

One

The Waters of Time

From inauspicious beginnings as a mere trickle in the Staffordshire Moorlands the River Trent slowly gathers pace. In the course of a meandering 171-mile journey to meet the Humber Estuary at Trent Falls near Alkborough it becomes a mighty waterway. Forty-two main tributaries and countless minor streams swell the flow. In England, only the River Severn carries a greater volume of water. Like all major rivers, the Trent historically fulfilled many roles: barrier, boundary, highway, trade corridor, and provider of resources.

Emerging on Biddulph Moor at a height of 900 feet above sea level, the headwaters descend over 400 feet in less than five miles to reach Norton Green. By the time the adolescent river leaves the Potteries conurbation it has plunged a further 130 feet. From Trentham, the river falls at a rate of around 10 feet per mile as far as its confluence with the River Sow. Here, the

1   *A sailing barge heads for Trent Falls on a favourable wind, c.1920. In the course of its journey to the sea from the Staffordshire Moorlands the Trent becomes a mighty tidal waterway.*

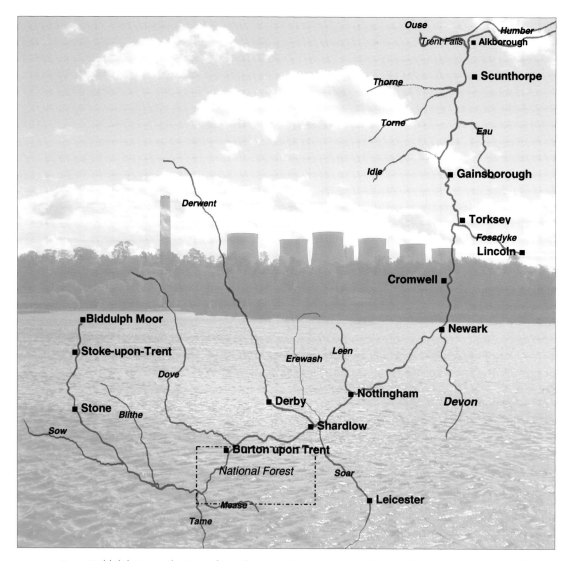

2   *From Biddulph Moor the Trent flows for 171 miles through the historically rich heart of England.*

flat floodplain that is a legacy of primordial post-glacial torrents slows the descent. A pattern of natural erosion and silt deposition results in sideways flows and looping meanders. Over time the neck of a meander may close, allowing the water to break through in a new channel and leaving behind a crescent-shaped lake known as an 'oxbow'. Following the flow downstream, a tendency to the right-hand side of the valley is noticeable. At many points the river brushes against hills on this flank, undercutting them

to create cliffs and steadily widen the broad vale.

In geological terms, the character of the Trent Valley is mainly Triassic, formed around 250 million years ago when the area was a marine environment. In the Pennine fringe of North Staffordshire there are outcrops of carboniferous limestone and millstone grit. Sandstone spurs occasionally make dramatic bluffs such as Castle Rock at Nottingham. Seabed deposits of Keuper marl, clay and shale mix with layers of Bunter pebble washed down in ancient rivers that once flowed from the north. In the shales are bands of calcium sulphate. In crystal form it is known as gypsum. As alabaster stone it can be worked and polished to produce a translucent, marmoreal finish. Water enriched by draining through the gypsum strata is particularly suitable for brewing beer. Carved alabaster and brewing both became flourishing industries in Nottinghamshire, Derbyshire and Staffordshire. Saline springs, a legacy of the area's marine geology, were exploited into the 20th century. Rich red clays were used to make bricks, tiles and domestic pottery. Gravel extraction continues as a large-scale commercial activity.

In Palaeolithic times, around 12,000 years ago, a re-configured landscape slowly emerged from the grip of an Ice Age. Glacial scouring re-routed rivers. Swollen by meltwater, powerful watercourses forged new channels, deep and wide through treeless arctic tundra. Trees began to re-colonise the land. Encouraged by the warming climate, oak, elm, hazel and lime followed birch and pine gradually northwards. Water loving alder and willow spread along riverbanks. An abundance of plant and animal life returned. As a natural communication route, the River Trent and its valley provided sites for early human settlements. Small hunter-gatherer bands camped on high gravel terraces. A flint scraper from Messingham, south of Scunthorpe, is among the rare traces of their presence so far discovered.

A wooden trackway and birch-branch platform discovered in a gravel quarry at Branston near Burton-on-Trent and a scatter of flint and chert tools from Misterton Carr (Nottinghamshire) are evidence that marshland in the Trent Valley was being exploited as long ago as 8000 B.C. Fish, wildfowl and reeds ensured a plentiful supply of food as well as material for thatching temporary shelters.

Neolithic enclosures and finds of flint tools, arrowheads and polished axeheads along the length of the river show the importance of the Trent as a trade highway in prehistory.

Clearance of the wildwood, begun in Neolithic times, continued into the Bronze Age. Early farmers sowed patches of emmer wheat and other crops in the fertile alluvial soil of the Trent Valley. With cultivation came settled communities. The first permanent structures appeared. Visible signs of occupation such as funerary barrow mounds where ancestors were laid to rest proclaimed territorial ownership. Erosion and ploughing has flattened many mounds leaving nothing but telltale crop marks visible on aerial photographs.

Investigation of a former river channel uncovered during sand and gravel extraction at Langford Lowfields, between Langford and Collingham, revealed 13 human crania and a number of animal skulls of late Neolithic/early Bronze-Age date. Apart from an occasional flint blade there were few associated finds and hardly any other bones. A tangle of brushwood and a fragment of wickerwork suggested a collapsed structure. Human skulls of a similar age have been found elsewhere in the Trent. A probable interpretation is that barrow burials were only for those of high status and the bodies of ordinary people were disposed of by exposure on a platform in the river. When only bones remained, the skulls were ritually deposited in the water.

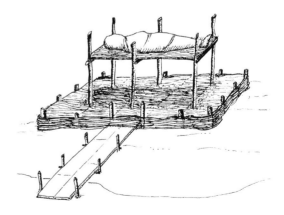

3 *Prehistoric finds suggest that bodies were disposed of by exposure on wooden platforms built in the river shallows. Decomposition 'freed the spirit' and bones were then placed in the water.*

Primitive boats preserved in river silt have been found along the length of the Trent from the Humber Estuary to Abbey Hulton in Stoke-on-Trent. Among the most exciting are a number of dugout log-boats, each carved from a single oak trunk. The transport capabilities of these simple but robust vessels was demonstrated by a cargo of quarried stone blocks still loaded aboard a log-boat discovered at Shardlow in 1998. Dendrochronology and radiocarbon dating techniques confirmed the craft to be 3,500 years old. Three log-boats and ancient timber revetments discovered at Clifton suggest the site of an important riverside settlement in the Bronze Age.

A few mounds containing fire-cracked stones and charcoal excavated from the silt of former river channels have proved difficult to interpret. Tool marks on timbers used to line troughs associated with the mounds are consistent with those produced by Bronze-Age axes. One of two burnt mounds uncovered in a quarry at Willington, Derbyshire contained a rectangular wooden trough of stout construction over six feet long and with a capacity of up to 88 gallons. Large stones found in the trough showed evidence of being heated in a fire before being plunged red hot into water. Cooking large joints of meat is the most likely practical explanation.

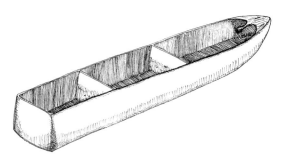

4   *A Bronze-Age log-boat, flat-bottomed in section and capable of carrying an estimated payload of one ton discovered at Shardlow was made from the trunk of a 400-year-old English oak. A knob-shaped protrusion inside the bow may have doubled as a cleat for tying up and a handle for portage.*

Small fragments of ox and horse bone bearing butchery marks were discovered at the site. An intriguing alternative theory is that the trough was the heart of a prehistoric sauna or steam room.

For much of its length the River Trent forms an administrative boundary dividing shire counties and civil parishes. For those who like to make such distinctions it is where the 'North' begins, that mythic smoke-blackened region of real ale, gritty authenticity, flat caps and even flatter vowels. Shire boundaries were largely set in place in the ninth century, an administrative response to the threat of Danish occupation. They overlie more ancient divisions. In Iron-Age Britain, the Trent divided the tribal territories of the *Corieltauvi* in the south and east from the *Cornovii* to the north and west.

The headwaters of the Trent can be crossed with a single stride but the river soon becomes a formidable barrier. Ancient trackways converged where it was possible for men and beasts to cross. Prehistoric Middle Street met the river at Burton Stather. Sewstern Lane crossed the Trent at Newark. Fords became a focus for trade. Control of such strategically important sites brought power. A hillfort at Bury Bank constructed in the second century B.C. commanded an ancient crossing at Meaford, near Stone. Earthworks – on Borough Hill overlooking a ford site at Walton-on-Trent, Brands Hill near Barton in Fabis, and on a ridge close to crossing points at Burton Joyce – enclosed hillforts or trading centres and possibly both. Roman goods were being imported along the Trent Valley a century before the conquest of Britain began in A.D. 43.

For nearly three decades the Trent defined the limits of Roman occupation. Native tribal strongholds including Bury Bank and a 20-acre hillfort on the summit of Breedon Hill, two miles south of the Trent in north-west Leicestershire, were abandoned. A line of fortresses was established along the Trent Valley to consolidate Roman authority before the legions pushed northwards. In Nottinghamshire, forts

5   *Rising behind the sinuous floodbank at Barton in Fabis is the wooded escarpment of Brandshill. An Iron-Age enclosure on the summit of Brands Hill was guarded by a series of parallel ditch and bank linear earthworks extending for half a mile.*

at *Segelocum* (Littleborough) and *Margidunum* (East Bridgford) controlled river crossings.

Some fords were only passable in favourable conditions. Others were more reliable. Frequently used crossings were paved to make passage easier. Stone setts ramped on oak pilings provided a sound base for a 20-ft wide causeway at Littleborough on the Roman road from Lincoln to Doncaster. There was a marching camp at Holme. A camp on the escarpment at Alkborough looking out over Trent Falls and the Humber Estuary would have been equipped with a watchtower. The *Antonine Itinerary*, a fourth-century route map of the Roman Empire, mentions a place called *Ad Pontem* ('near the bridge') midway between *Margidunum* and *Crococalana* (Brough), indicating the presence

of a bridge in Roman times close to Thorpe and East Stoke. Garrisons at Marton and Newton on Trent were probably home to the IXth Legion. A Roman road crossed the Trent at Sawley in Derbyshire linking the Fosse Way to Ryknield Street. A camp recorded as *Ad Trivonam* stood near a ford between South Derbyshire and East Staffordshire. A possible Roman fort has been identified guarding the river crossing at Hanford, Stoke-on-Trent. *Sandonium* has been identified with Sandon in Staffordshire and *Rutunium* with Stone. Crop marks west of the river at Aston-by-Stone point to a possible Roman camp. Foundations of a Roman building lie beneath Southwell Minster. Trentside villas have been identified at Barton in Fabis, Thurgaton, Cromwell, and

IMP CAES
MARCO
PIA ONO
VICTORI
NO FP
INV
AUG PON
MAX
TRP PP
ALS · M
P XIIII

6 *A third-century Roman milestone from Lincoln helps to identify Littleborough as* Segelocum, *an important river crossing. Politically inspired abbreviated Latin translates as: Under Emperor Marcus Piavonius Victorinus [Gallic emperor A.D. 269-70] dutiful, pious, and invincible Augustus, chief pontiff with tribunal power, father of the people. From* Lindum *(Lincoln) to* Segelocum *14 [Roman] miles.*

Winterton. At Littleborough, ploughing has turned up coins spanning four centuries of Roman rule. In 1979, a hoard of Roman coins was found in Jolpool Brook, Burston close to where the stream empties into the Trent. A Roman pottery kiln from the first century was uncovered close to the river at Trent Vale in North Staffordshire. At the other end of the Trent, Roman kilns have been identified at Lea, south of Gainsborough. Pottery, coins and other finds indicate a Romano-British settlement at Hardwick Hill on the edge of Scotton Com-

mon. Slag from this site suggests an early iron foundry. A settlement occupied from the Iron Age into Roman times has been excavated on a river terrace at Rampton.

Although there is little hard evidence for Roman use of river transport it was almost certainly more extensive than most historians allow. Those famously direct Roman roads were primarily to enable the legions to march across country quickly. Moving cargo by water would have been speedier and safer than using waggons yoked to oxen or horses. Roman technology certainly extended to engineering canal systems. The Fossdyke, an 11-mile waterway between Torksey and Lincoln, was created in the second century by linking an arm of the River Till and a small tributary of the Trent. This cutting enabled access between the important Roman towns of Lincoln, Doncaster and York via the Trent, Don and Ouse. Lead, subject to an Empire monopoly, was transported as 'pigs' or ingots. A pig smelted in Derbyshire was discovered at Brough (Roman *Petvaria*) on the north bank of the Humber. If export was via the Humberside ports, ingots may well have been shipped along the Trent by barge.

From the writings of Tacitus comes a suggestion that the river was known to the Romans as *Trisantona*. This has been translated by some as 'trespasser', a reference to frequent flooding. *Treanta*, *Treenta*, *Treonta*, and *Trenta* all appear in early-medieval documents. A colourful alternative explanation links the name with Late Latin *trentale* meaning thirty. An old rhyme claims, 'The beauteous Trent enseams thirty kinds of fish and thirty different streams'. According to John Milton, the river 'Like some earth born giant spreads his thirty arms along the indented meads'. A more plausible derivation is that the name derives from a contraction of Anglo-British *the-re-hemm-heth* or 'the river bend landing place'. It may originally have applied to a particular reach, possibly Trentham in North Staffordshire, and later extended to the river itself. The name *Trenth* occurs in 13th-century documents.

7   *A Humber keel at Drinsey Nook on the Fossdyke heading for Lincoln (c.1905). The Fossdyke was engineered in the second century by linking an arm of the River Till to a tributary of the Trent.*

8 A list from 1641 of fish in the Trent includes crayfish (a crustacean) and 'dates' (probably freshwater mussels); 'whitling' (young bull trout); 'smelts' (salmon); 'pinkes' (minnows or salmon parr); 'chevin' (chub); 'pickerel' (pike); and 'ruff' (perch family). 'Shad', related to herring, travel upriver to spawn.

Anglo-Saxon language and fashions were imported across the North Sea in post-Roman Britain. The settlement or *burh* of a tribal group of Angles known as the *Gainas* is said to have given Gainsborough its name. Cultural change and continental ideas spread along the Trent Valley. Excavations at Brough revealed an extensive Anglo-Saxon community. A cemetery in use for more than two hundred years from the fifth century has been uncovered at Holme Pierrepont. At Millgate, Newark, between the old Fosse Way and the river, a large pagan cemetery of similar age contained mostly cremated remains buried in pottery urns. At the edge of the site, in an elevated position looking out over the Trent, an enclosure ditch surrounded the grave of a woman who died in early middle age *c.*600. Rich grave goods, including coins, a bronze-trimmed wooden bucket, and jewellery of bronze, silver, amber, and glass, led to speculation that she was an Anglo-Saxon princess.

Lindsey, now a division of Lincolnshire; and Mercia, wrapped around the River Trent in the central Midlands, were two of the politically distinct mini-kingdoms into which post-Roman England devolved. Lindsey became a pawn in a battle for dominance between Mercia and

Northumbria. The Anglo-Saxon scholar and theologian, Bede, records that in 679 a great battle was fought near the River Trent between King Ecgfrith of Northumbria and Aethelred, King of the Mercians. Victory for Aethelred made Lindsey part of Mercia.

Raids by Scandinavian Vikings who used the river as an invasion route were a constant threat during the ninth century. In 868, a force dug in for the winter at Nottingham. A Danish army camped at Torksey in 872, moving inland the following year to sack Nottingham before pushing further into the heart of Mercia. Church treasures were looted and monasteries at Breedon and Repton destroyed. Around two and a half thousand warriors spent the winter of 873/4 at Repton, their longships docked below the bluff occupied by the monastic buildings. Settlers followed, migrating along the Trent and spreading along its tributaries. By the 10th century, the Trent in Staffordshire marked the limits of Anglo-Saxon territory and a separate administrative region known as the Danelaw.

Nottingham and Lincoln on navigable waterways were two of five administrative centres set up under Scandinavian rule. The impact of Norse colonisation in the East Midlands is reflected in the predominance of villages with

9 *A Viking army moored their longships during the winter of 874/5 on this old arm of the river at Repton close to a Saxon monastic site now occupied by St Wystan's Church.*

10 *Named after the Norse god of the oceans, the aegir (pictured here at Morton) is a tidal bore or wave created when a high incoming tide meets the outward flowing river current.*

the Scandinavian place name suffixes –*by* (often near to Roman roads or ancient trackways) and –*thorpe* (frequently combined with a personal name element). Settlements with the common Old English –ton suffix (meaning farm or village) were transformed to sound Scandinavian. An example is Carlton-on-Trent, that would have been Charlton to speakers of Anglo-Saxon. A proliferation of 'gate' street names (from the Norse *gata* for 'road'), most noticeably at Newark and Nottingham, is another etymological Viking legacy. The Trent's tidal bore, a predictable wave phenomenon created by a high incoming tide meeting the downstream flow of the river, is named after Aegir, Norse god of the oceans.

An invasion force led by Sweyn Forkbeard, King of Denmark, sailed along the Trent in 1013, mooring at Morton and camping on Thonock Hill. Sweyn's sovereignty was soon acknowledged in the Danelaw. A series of victories against Anglo-Saxon armies made him virtually ruler of England. Sweyn's sudden death in 1014 at Gainsborough sparked Anglo-Saxon resurgence led by King Aethelred and his son Edmund Ironside. It was brief. Both men were dead by 1016. Sweyn's son Cnut reasserted Danish power and was crowned king of a unified England the following year. Some locate the legend of Cnut demonstrating the limits of his kingly powers against the tide at Gainsborough.

A crudely incised longship on the stonework of a pier in the chancel arch at St Mary's, Stow-in-Lindsey is believed to date from the early 11th century. If, as seems likely, the carving is the work of a warrior who sailed with Sweyn Forkbeard, it is the earliest depiction of a Viking longship in England.

The river was a vital resource. Weirs harnessed the power of the current to drive simple, horizontal mill wheels and exploit fish stocks. The Domesday inventory of 1086 gives a clear indication of the importance of the River Trent to the economy of the period. Only nine boroughs – fortified towns with ancient liberties and privileges that enabled them to become commercial centres – are recorded in the whole of Staffordshire, Derbyshire, Leicestershire, Nottinghamshire and Lincolnshire. Three of these boroughs, Nottingham, Newark and Torksey, owed their status largely to location on the Trent. All were the sites of royal mints in the 10th and 11th centuries. A mint at Nottingham operated until 1154. Lincoln, also a borough and with approximately six thousand inhabitants by far the largest, benefited hugely from its access to the Trent via Torksey and the Fossdyke.

11   *A Viking longship roughly scratched on a pier of the chancel arch at St Mary's Church, Stow-in-Lindsey may date from the invasion of Sweyn Forkbeard in 1013.*

Domesday Book records numerous fisheries and mills along the Trent, most of them belonging either to the Crown or the Church. Over time, more efficient vertical mill wheels were introduced. Hedge weirs were used to divert water into millraces. From the 13th century wool production grew in scale and many corn mills were converted for fulling. Fish weirs, constructed of woven hazel or willow hurdles fixed between stakes driven into the river bed, were in common use from Anglo-Saxon times. Artificial barriers funnelled fish into nets or cone-shaped wicker baskets that allowed fish to enter but prevented their escape. As a fishing method it was indiscriminate and potentially harmful to overall stocks. Enormous catches of eels and lampreys were taken during spring migration. Stake alignments and partially preserved wattle hurdles have been discovered in the river at Colwick, Clifton, Dunham on Trent, Holme Pierrepont and elsewhere. A tapered wicker fish trap was discovered preserved by the anaerobic river silt in a Trentside quarry at Hemington in north-west Leicestershire.

Wildfowl and geese were hunted and trapped for the table. Swans have been claimed as royal birds by monarchs from medieval times. Licences, known as 'royalties', were granted, permitting important Trentside landowners to take swans for the table. Cygnets were rounded up in late autumn and branded with distinctive beak notches. Birds frequently had their wings clipped to prevent them straying too far. Where birds from different stretches mated, the fledglings were divided. In Tudor times, roast swan was a prized menu item. Along with goose, it was a popular choice for Christmas banquets. Swan down was used in bedding and primary feathers were generally acknowledged as making the finest quill pens.

Although pottery was a significant local industry into the 13th century, Torksey chiefly relied on river trade and the business generated by Lincoln. Decline was apparent at the time of the Domesday survey which records 213 burgesses before 1066 had reduced to 102 in

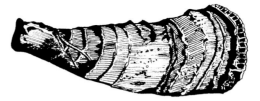

12   *Wicker fish trap of the type discovered at Colwick preserved in the silt of the riverbed.*

Iɴ *Torcheseɣ*. T.R.E. fueꝛ̃. cc.7 xɪɪɪ. burgenſes. Eaſdē c̄ſuetudines habebant om̄s q̃s & Lincolienſes. 7 tantū plus qđ q̃cunq̃ eoꝛ̃ manſionē in ead uilla habebat. neq̃ intrans neq̃ exiens theloneū dabat nec c̄ſuetudinē. Hoc aut̃ eoꝛ̃ erat. ut ſi legati regis illuc ueniren̄ꝛ̃⁖ hōes ej̃d uici cū nauibꝛ̃ ſuis 7 alijs inſtrum̄tis nauigationis uſq̃ eboracū eos conduce reꝛ̃.7 uicecomes uict̃u legatoꝛ̃ 7 nautaru ex firma ſua inueniret. Qđ ſi aliq̃s burgenſiū alibi uellet abire.7 domū quæ ẽt in ead uilla uendere⁖ ſine ſcientia ꝓpoſiti ſi uellet poſſet facere.

Hcc ſuburbiū Torcheſÿg 7 Harduic M̃ ei c̄tiguū habuit Eddid regina in dñio.7 habeꝺ foris urbē .ɪɪ. car træ ſine geldo. Modo h̄ꝛ̃ rex in dñio.7 ſuꝛ̃ ibi. cɪɪ. burgenſes manentes. Waſtæ ſuꝛ̃ ū. c.xɪ. manſiones. Ad hanc uillā ꝑtin̄ xx. ac̃ pti.7 ʟx. ac̃ ſiluæ minutæ.7 xɪ. piſcariæ. Vna ex his.ē Bereng̃ de tcdeni. T.R.E. int̃ regē 7 comitē. ual̃. xvɪɪɪ. liꝺ. m̃.xxx. liꝺ.

T.R.E. reddeꝺ Torcheſiÿ 7 Harduic in Lincolia q̃ntū denarrū de geldo ciuitatis. Ad hāc q̃ntā parte dabat Torcheſÿg. ɪɪ. den.7 Harduic tciū. De hac Torcheſig habebat Morcar tciū denariū de om̄ibꝛ̃ c̄ſuetudiniꝺ.

In Harduic h̄ꝺ Suen 7 Godric. ɪ. car træ.7 ibi ma nebant. xɪɪ. hōes. Modo h̄ꝛ̃ Roger de buſli me dietatē.7 eꝑs Lincolienſis aliā med. ad S̃ ᴍᴀʀɪᴀ de Stou. Ibi cadit tcia pars geldi regis. qđ rex ñ h̄ꝛ̃ de illa q̃ ꝑtin ad Dorcheſÿg.

13   *Domesday Book records the decline of Torksey since the Norman Conquest. Two hundred and thirteen burgesses have reduced to 102 and 111 houses (*mansiones*) are empty (*wastae*). Freedom from certain tolls is confirmed in return for providing a ship to carry the king's officials (*legati regis*) to York (*eboracu[m]*) on demand. Eleven fisheries (*piscariae*) are recorded as belonging to the town.*

14 *A tug tows four dumb barges towards Trent Falls. There are panoramic views of the Trent as it nears the Humber Estuary from the hills between Burton upon Stather and Alkborough.*

the two decades since the Conquest. Torksey's burgesses enjoyed considerable freedoms in return for providing a boat for any of the king's officers requiring transport to York.

Management of the river intensified as its importance as a trade route grew. The Fossdyke, which had fallen out of use after the end of Roman occupation, was dredged, repaired and re-opened in 1121. Revetments at particularly vulnerable sites protected the riverbank from erosion. A series of projecting triangular jetties made of oak pilings filled with sandstone were added in the 14th century, close to the confluence with the River Derwent to protect the riverbank and speed the flow of water.

The prosperity of Gainsborough, Newark and Nottingham in the medieval period was closely linked to their importance as river ports. In 1298, the bailiffs of Gainsborough were given permission for a quay tax to raise money for improvements. Soon after, Gainsborough gained the privilege of being nominated as a port through which grain for the royal household

was supplied. Obstruction of vessels on the Trent was a recurring problem. Hefty fines were enforced on weirs that hindered river traffic. The rule of thumb, confirmed in a charter granted by Henry II to the borough of Nottingham *c*.1155, specified no weir should be erected within a perch (a measure of approximately 16½ ft) of midstream. The charter also gave the burgesses of Nottingham the right to levy tolls on boats using the river between Thrumpton and Newark. Article 33 of *Magna Carta*, signed in 1215, has a clause demanding the removal of kydells (weirs) on all rivers to ensure free passage for boats. In 1322, Edward II appointed a Crown official to safeguard the movement of boats and their cargoes on the Trent. Further protection followed in 1332 when Edward III issued a proclamation preventing landowners charging for boats that had to be towed from the banks across their estates.

Diversion of the Trent to drive a mill owned by the Byron family, lords of the manor at Colwick, triggered a long-running dispute. In 1330, a deal was struck allowing boats bound for Trent Bridge Wharf at Nottingham to moor up at Colwick when water levels were low and for packhorses and carts to have access over the Colwick Estates. It was an unsatisfactory compromise. In 1392 an official inquiry upheld complaints that too much water was being drawn into the millstream at Colwick, and that osier beds and a fish weir were obstructing river traffic.

A Royal Commission was convened in 1347 to adjudicate after a channel dug to provide power for mills owned by the Sutton lords of the manor at Averham and Kelham had been widened to a point that made navigation through Newark difficult. By 1558, the Kelham cut had become the main waterway. Mill owners in Newark had to apply through the courts for a weir to be installed at Averham to ensure sufficient water supply.

Domestic freight included corn, coal, cheese, butter, fish and salt. Nottingham, Newark and Gainsborough also acted as collection points for wool, the product of numerous monastic granges, destined for export to Florence and other rich European cultural and commercial centres. Both Hull and Boston acted as exit ports. Goods destined for Boston were either sent overland from Newark or along the Fossdyke via Torksey to the River Witham.

Markets and fairs were generally restricted to boroughs where legal trading times could be enforced and basic consumer protection exercised. A thriving market based on river traffic that developed at Burton upon Stather received an official confirmatory charter in 1314. Fairs and markets held under the authority of the Bishop of Lincoln were moved from Stow to Marton to take advantage of a riverside site. The number of Trentside towns and villages with market charters grew rapidly in the 13th and 14th centuries.

Alabaster deposits in south Derbyshire and east Staffordshire were being extensively quarried from the 14th century, most notably at Chellaston from where stone could be easily carried along the Trent to workshops in Nottingham and Burton-on-Trent. Almost translucent and easy to work, it was an ideal sculptural medium. Schools of skilled craftsmen produced lifelike monumental effigies of the highest quality for customers throughout England and for export to Europe. Lead from the Derbyshire Peak District was sent by packhorse to Bawtry for carriage along the River Idle to the Trent at Stockwith.

Fords, situated where there were natural shallows, were common along the River Trent and often remained in use even when a bridge

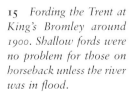

15 *Fording the Trent at King's Bromley around 1900. Shallow fords were no problem for those on horseback unless the river was in flood.*

16   *A horse and cart crossing on Walkerith chain ferry in the 1900s.*

was built alongside. The expense of maintaining a bridge might mean use was restricted to when flooding made the ford impassable. Generally 'shallow' meant less than waist high, not too much of a problem for those on horseback. Prudent travellers carried a staff to test water depth.

The more traffic used a crossing, the more likely it was that a bridge would eventually be built on the site. Place-names, for example: Twyford (two fords); Shelford (shallow ford); Strongford; Spalford; and Hazelford identify sites. In rural areas, clues to old crossings can be found on maps where public rights of way converge on opposite banks of the river. In urban areas, most traces of ancient fords have

vanished over time, obscured by multiple layers of construction.

Ferries, often subject to a manorial monopoly, provided a more convenient and reliable alternative to fords. In the deep tidal reaches of the lower Trent they were a practical necessity. Small boats or flat-bottomed punts were rowed, poled, or hauled across on a cable fed between vertical rollers to a winding drum. Occasionally a horse might be harnessed to a winch mechanism. Where demand existed, larger boats capable of carrying a few head of livestock or a pony and trap were used. Landing stages provided good opportunities for exchanging gossip and ferry operators were usually well informed on local affairs.

In *WESTVNE* .hb Algar .x. car̄ tre 7 ii. bou 7 dim ad glđ.
Tra totiđ car̄. Ibi nc̄ in dn̄io .iii. car̄ .7 xxiiii. uilti .7 vi. borđ.
hn̄tes .xii. car̄ .7 iiii. cenſarij redđ .xvi. ſol. Ibi .ii. æcclæ 7 pbr.
7 i. molin̄ .xix. ſoliđ 7 iiii. den̄ .7 piſcina 7 paſſagiu aquæ .xiii.
ſol 7 iiii. den̄ .7 li. ac̄ p̄ti. Paſcua dimiđ lev lḡ .7 iii. q̄ʒ lat.
T.R.E. uat̄ .vii. lib̄. m̄. vi. lib̄.   Ber huj m̄.

17   *The Domesday survey for Weston-on-Trent includes a mill* (molin); *fishpond* (piscina); *and a ferry* (passagiu aquae). *The ferry is valued at 13s. 4d.* (xiii sol[idus] iiii den[arii]).

In the late 11th century when Domesday Book was compiled, a ferry at Littleborough was a vital link on the main road from Lincoln to Doncaster and York. Ferries (*passagiu aquae*) are also recorded in the Domesday inventory at Fiskerton (property of Archbishop Thomas and serving Southwell), Gunthorpe, Lea and Weston-on-Trent. The earliest mention in historical records for most ferries occurs later. A 13th-century deed of Shelford Priory records a grant of the rights of Gunthorpe Ferry to the monks of Thurgaton Priory. Laneham Ferry is documented in 1251. A ferry at Gainsborough is recorded in 1281. Marnham Ferry first appears in the Patent Rolls of 1316: by 1619 there was sufficient traffic to keep three boats employed. In Lincolnshire, services ran at various times between East Ferry and Owston Ferry; Burringham and Althorpe; and Burton Stather and Garthorpe. Between Lincolnshire and Nottinghamshire there were ferries from

Walkerith to Walkeringham; East Stockwith to West Stockwith; Lea to Bole; Marton to Littleborough; Laughterton to Laneham; and Newton on Trent to Dunham on Trent. Elsewhere in Nottinghamshire, ferries operated from Fledborough; Marnham; Sutton on Trent; Carlton-on-Trent; North Muskham; Farndon; Fiskerton; Hazelford; Hoveringham; Gunthorpe; Stoke Bardolph; Radcliffe on Trent; Colwick; Wilford; Barton in Fabis; and Thrumpton. In Derbyshire, there were crossings at Sawley; Weston-on-Trent (at King's Mills); Shardlow; Twyford; Willington; and from Stapenhill to Burton-on-Trent in Staffordshire. The first mention of Willington Ferry, saving a detour of 20 miles to reach its neighbour Repton on the opposite bank, does not occur until 1600. A penny paid for the crossing is noted in Repton's churchwarden accounts. Most ferry services were probably established long before the first records appear.

18   *Hoveringham Ferry, one of many small boats that operated passenger services between settlements along the river.*

By the beginning of the 20th century, many ferries had ceased. Few of those remaining survived the next fifty years. The last ferryman at King's Mills was Polly Rowbottom, who wound a boat capable of carrying horses but not carts across the river on a chain. It was not uncommon for women to operate ferryboats. Women ran two of the last regular commercial Trent crossings at Thrumpton and Farndon.

Accidents were a random hazard. In the 1930s, the King's Mills boat broke free and was swept downstream to Shardlow. Stockwith Ferry once broke loose with a horsedrawn omnibus on board. A barge holed and sank Littleborough Ferry, bringing an abrupt end to the service in the early 20th century. Half-a-dozen cows being taken for milking on the Mering Ferry at Sutton on Trent moved to one side of the flat-bottomed boat causing it to capsize. The cattle swam safely to the bank. Farmer Asher drowned. The ferryman and two passengers lost their lives when the aegir swamped Owston

Ferry. In 1784, six passengers drowned when Wilford Ferry capsized in gale-force winds. Six died when Gainsborough Ferry overturned in 1760.

Today there are around seventy bridges across the Trent. They come in all shapes and sizes, from narrow footbridges to six-lane motorway carriages, and in a variety of designs and materials. The first bridges across the Trent were flat-decked timber walkways stretched between stone piers. Bases for piers were made of iron-tipped wooden piles driven deep into the riverbed and surrounded with a stone-filled platform or 'starling' to protect against scour and debris. An obstruction, removed during improvements to the Navigation in 1884 at the Oven, south of Cromwell near the site of an ancient ford to Collingham, turned out to be bases for bridge piers. Vestiges of stout oak piles were uncovered, secured within lozenge-shaped timber shuttering filled with limestone rubble. Originally the bases were thought to belong

19 *First World War volunteers on a pontooning course at Fiskerton in 1915 learn how to build a bridge of boats. The riverside camp was frequently flooded.*

20 *Bridge building techniques from the 14th century onwards are revealed in the stonework of old Walton Bridge at Stone. Originally a narrow pack-horse bridge, it was subject to several phases of widening and rebuilding before it was replaced in 1984 by a new bridge built alongside.*

to a Roman bridge. Modern dating techniques applied to surviving sections of timber revealed an eighth-century felling date.

A better understanding of civil engineering, and masonry skills honed on building the great cathedrals of Norman England, led to the introduction of stone arches. Semicircular or 'barrel' vaults distribute weight equally across the full width of an arch. Ribbed arches, a technical innovation borrowed from 12th-century church architecture, made construction easier. Individual ribs transfer downward thrust laterally and remove the need for the whole arch to be self-supporting. Pointed Gothic arches provided boats with more headroom but were narrower and required additional supporting piers that

interfered with the flow of the river and created eddies. Starlings developed into wedge-shaped cutwaters that were often extended to the parapet to form pedestrian refuges. From the 14th century, 'segmental' arches began to appear. Their flatter profile, part of a circle as with barrel vaults but a smaller segment of a much larger circle, allowed wide arches to be built. On low-lying approaches, causeways were as important as bridges and were engineered using the same techniques, with arches for flood relief.

Remnants of an ancient bridge, possibly medieval, discovered at Great Haywood in 1938 were not fully investigated. At Hemington Fields quarry the remains of three medieval bridges have been studied in detail. The earliest proved to be a unique late 11th-century timber structure, the last a 13th-century stone bridge. Bronze-Age and Iron-Age settlements discovered on a line north and south of this crossing near the confluence with the River Derwent point to a significant routeway in prehistoric times.

A timber bridge at Newark, built in 1135 by Bishop Alexander of Lincoln, was authorised by Henry I on condition 'That it may not hurt my city of Lincoln or my borough of Nottingham'. An additional clause demonstrating the economic importance of the Trent as a trade route was comparable with the Fosse Way and Great North Road.

Often, the first documentary evidence for a bridge is a grant of pontage, the authority allowing a tax to be levied on travellers in order to pay for essential repairs. Maintenance of bridges was a constant problem. Many medieval bridges had tenements and shops built on them and rents were applied to the upkeep of the struc-

ture. Until a succession of widening schemes implemented in the 17th and 18th centuries, many bridges were only wide enough for foot passengers or horses. Travellers by coach were required to alight and walk across the bridge while carriages forded the river.

Before the signing of *Magna Carta*, the state required two main duties of all freemen: to give military service and undertake bridge repairs when called upon. After 1215, responsibility was assigned to an individual or an administrative group such as a hundred, riding, borough, town, or parish. Shire counties became accountable only by default. Liabilities were frequently disputed. Justices of the Peace were authorised to investigate cases of neglect at quarter sessions and had the power to enforce action or impose a tax to pay for repairs. County Councils took over from the courts after the local government reforms of 1888 and in the years that followed almost all privately owned bridges on public highways transferred into public ownership.

Two

Down to the River to Pray

In prehistoric times nature was regarded as a physical reflection of the spiritual world. The Trent was part of a sacred landscape, worshipped as a deity. Confluence points, where tributaries joined the main flow, were particularly revered. Ritual sites, including a timber henge monument built by some of the first farmers around five thousand years ago at Fatholme in East Staffordshire, have been identified along the Trent Valley. A banked avenue or 'cursus' over one mile long at Aston-on-Trent in Derbyshire is believed to represent a symbolic river.

A variety of weapons, including beautifully wrought swords in the European Hallstatt cultural style of 900-500 B.C. have been found in the Trent at Fiskerton, Newark, Holme Pierrepont, Clifton, Attenborough and elsewhere. These incredibly valuable items, the equivalent of a luxury car today, were not accidental losses but deliberate deposits, indicative of votive offerings to placate or influence the gods.

Steps leading to the foundations of a circular building, discovered in the 19th century on a hillside overlooking the Trent at Thrumpton, suggest the site of a Roman temple. Two Roman altars have been unearthed at Littleborough.

A Roman origin is claimed for a rare turf maze at Alkborough, one of only a few such monuments to survive in England. Known as Julian's Bower, it is named after the son of Aeneas. According to classical mythology, Aeneas founded Rome on his divinely inspired travels after the Trojan War. Sweeping views from the limestone ridge of the Humber, Trent and Ouse confluence, extending beyond to the Yorkshire Wolds and Derbyshire's Peak District, would have made the maze site a special place from early times. Sacred sites have a history of continuity. A much worn Saxon cross of millstone grit in the churchyard at Alkborough testifies to early Christian preaching in the area. Saxon masonry survives in the lower part of the church tower and Roman foundations lie beneath. Fragments of stonework from a Roman military camp are incorporated in an arch leading from the tower to the nave.

21 *Beautifully forged prehistoric iron and bronze swords found in the river may have been deliberately deposited as ritual offerings. Some are in the distinctive Hallstatt cultural style found across northern Europe with a 'mushroom' pommel and long, lancet-shaped blades ending in a 90-degree point.*

22 *A stone altar is among a number of finds from the Roman period uncovered near the river crossing between Littleborough and Marton.*

The first written record of the maze does not appear until 1697. A cell of monks attached to the priory at Spalding, founded by Countess Lucy of Chester (*c.*1070-*c.*1139) and her husband Ivo Taillebois, may have been responsible for laying out the maze in the 12th century. Lucy, a wealthy heiress, had strong family connections with the area and the earthworks of a fortified manor house at Countess Close, Alkborough are associated with her. For Christians in the Middle Ages the winding path portrayed a route to salvation, a penitential alternative to pilgrimage for those in search of redemption. An iron model of Julian's Bower is set in the porch floor of nearby St John's Church.

A fanciful, royal connection is possible. Geoffrey Plantagenet, illegitimate son of Henry II, was appointed Bishop of Lincoln in 1173 and was probably the man who rebuilt Newark Castle in stone. His mother was rumoured to be Jane Clifford, referred to by King Henry as 'My fair Rosamund'. For Jane's protection, Henry built a house called *Labyrinthus,* 'Like unto a knot in a garden called a maze'. A jealous Queen Eleanor is said to have gained access by following a thread to plant poison and murder her husband's mistress. No shred of evidence for the story exists beyond the word of Higden of Chester, a 14th-century monk, but could the maze be a medieval memorial?

23 *Julian's Bower, Alkborough is a rare surviving example of the turf mazes popular in Tudor and Stuart England. Maze patterns were used by the early Church to symbolise the path to salvation. Alkborough maze is similar to Christian designs in medieval France.*

24 *Fragments of Saxon masonry confirm the presence of a riverside church on the site of St Wilfrid's, Wilford long before the present building. A ford here may have been used for early-Christian baptisms.*

Christianity, introduced to Roman Britain in the second and third centuries, retained a tenuous hold in the fifth and sixth centuries largely due to the evangelical efforts of Irish missionaries who travelled along the Trent preaching the gospel. Pope Gregory, concerned at the increasing doctrinal differences between the Church of Rome and Celtic orthodoxy, sent his own religious delegation in 597. Under the leadership of Augustine, who became the first Archbishop of Canterbury, dioceses were created. Augustine's right-hand man Paulinus was consecrated Bishop of York. In 627, when full immersion was the order of the day, Paulinus is said to have performed a mass baptism in the waters of the Trent near a place St Bede calls *Tiowulfingacæstir*, identified by some with Littleborough and by others with Newark. Wilfrid (634-709) performed similar baptismal ceremonies. It is likely that Wilford (possibly a contraction of 'Wilfrid's Ford') was the scene of such an event. Saxon masonry built into the porch and walls of the south aisle of St Wilfrid's Church at Wilford, indicates a consecrated building long before the present riverside church.

Early missionaries set up preaching crosses and portable altars at open air meeting places. Churches followed. Religion was formalised. People no longer found their gods in nature. Paulinus is said to have founded a church at Southwell, but the current minster has its origins in a gift of land by King Edwy in the early 950s.

An Irish nun, Modwen, is credited with bringing the seeds of faith to Burton-on-Trent on her way to Rome. According to legend she established a church dedicated to St Andrew on an island in the Trent known today as Andresey (Andrew's Isle). Returning from her pilgrimage, she founded a second church at the foot of a hill on the opposite, eastern bank of the river. A 16th-century text tells that Modwen was in contact with a hermit called Hardulche who lived not far away in a rocky Trentside cell. Two nuns sent to collect a book from the hermit's cell became the subjects of a tale of divine intervention after their boat overturned in a storm. It was said that when Modwen and Hardulche set off to search for the missing women, the waters of the Trent miraculously parted, leading them to the fateful spot. Hardulche and his cell by the river may be the stuff of legend but the caves of Anchor Church, beside a backwater 10 miles downstream of Burton-on-Trent, provide a suitable dramatic backdrop.

Conversion in the Midlands gathered impetus with the baptism of Peada, Prince of Mercia in 653 following his marriage to Ahlflaed, daughter of the Christian king of Northumbria, Oswy. A double monastery housing monks and nuns was established shortly afterwards, overlooking the Trent at Repton. From Repton, the monks spread the Christian message along the river, founding a church close to a crossing point at Sawley. By the early ninth century, the church at Sawley had developed into a wealthy adjunct of the See of Lichfield.

Peada's brief reign was followed by a period of Northumbrian hegemony before his younger brothers Wulfhere and Aethelred reasserted Mercian independence. Chad, a Northumbrian monk who had studied under St Aidan, became Bishop of Mercia in 669 at the invitation of Wulfhere.

The one-and-a-half-hectare hillfort on Bury Bank, strategically placed above the river crossing at Meaford, was reoccupied in Anglo-Saxon times. It may be *Wulfherecaster*, location of a seventh-century Mercian royal hall, or possibly *Tricengeham*, site of a nunnery headed by Wulfhere's daughter, Werburgh, and recorded in the *Chartulary of Chester Abbey*. 'Nuns' Walk', a path on Bury Bank, leads to Tittensor Church. *Tricengeham* has also been identified with Threekingham in Lincolnshire and with Trentham in Staffordshire.

According to tradition, Wulfhere reverted to paganism and murdered his sons Wulfad and Ruffin after they met the future St Chad and converted to Christianity. A stone cairn raised over the princes' grave by their mother Ermenilda is said to give the town of Stone its name. History records that Wulfhere only had one son, Coenred, and almost certainly remained a practising Christian all his life. An early church dedicated to St Wulfad was established near the Trent at Stone where it is claimed Wulfhere was buried. When Geoffrey de Clinton bought the land from Enisan de Walton in 1122 to endow a priory for the Augustinian order, reference was made to an existing convent of nuns. Legend survives in the dedication of Stone parish church to St Michael and St Wulfad; and at Burston, where one version of the myth claims Rufin was slain. Redbrick St Rufin's Chapel at Burston was built in 1859, replacing an earlier building that has since disappeared.

Under the direction of King Aethelred of Mercia, during the last quarter of the seventh century, a monastery on the former fortified hilltop at Breedon was endowed. A wealthy

25 *Early-Christian hermits have been associated with the caves known as 'Anchor Church' near Foremark. Doors, visible in this old photograph, have since been removed. They were originally fitted in the 18th century by local squire Sir Robert Burdett, who converted Anchor Church into an exotic venue to wine and dine guests.*

26 *There has been a church by the crossing at Sawley since Saxon times. A stone bridge and causeway that replaced the ferry around 1500 was rebuilt in the 18th century and superseded by an iron span in the 1900s.*

Anglo-Saxon settlement has been excavated at Flixborough on a west-facing ridge looking out over the Trent. The layout of the buildings suggests a monastic site with a church at the centre.

'Stow' and 'Stoke' derive from the Anglo-Saxon word 'stoc' meaning at its simplest 'place'. Usually the connotation is 'holy place'. In the seventh century, the gospel was preached at the confluence of the Trent and Fowlea Brook, now the centre of Stoke-upon-Trent. A stone church followed an earlier wooden shelter at the beginning of the ninth century.

St Guthred became a hermit as penance for killing a man in an argument over a woman. He claimed to have been cured of leprosy by drinking water from the well of St Catherine, on what is now Sconce Hills, overlooking the Trent at Newark. Traditionally, his hermitage was where Old Hall, in Millgate next to Holy Trinity Church, was later built.

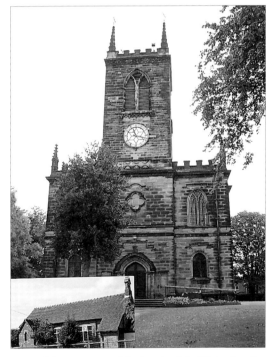

27 *The present parish church of St Michael and St Wulfad, Stone was consecrated in 1758. An earlier, Saxon church became part of the priory of St Mary and St Wulfad. A tiny redbrick church at nearby Burston (inset) is dedicated to Wulfad's brother, St Rufin.*

28 *St Mary's Church, Stow-in-Lindsey, built by a Saxon bishop whose diocese stretched from of the Humber to the Thames.*

29 *A beautiful cruciform Saxon crypt (inset), the mausoleum of the kings of Mercia, survived destruction when a Viking army sacked the Trentside monastic site at Repton in 874. In 1779, a workman digging a grave beneath the chancel floor of St Wystan's Church rediscovered the crypt by accident.*

A minster or 'mother' church at Stow-in-Lindsey, serving the spiritual needs of a far-flung rural community, was created in the late 10th century when Lincoln became part of the Diocese of Leicester. The site, on the road approaching the ford from Marton to Littleborough, is traditionally where Etheldreda (*c.*630-79), founder of a monastery at Ely, rested during a journey to Northumbria. When Etheldreda's ash staff was thrust into the ground it is said to have sprouted, providing her with instant shelter. Stow has been identified with *Sidnacester,* cathedral centre of Lindsey established in 677 when the see was separated from Lindisfarne by King Ecgfrith. If so, any church would most probably have been a wooden structure like most Anglo-Saxon buildings and destroyed without trace by one of the Viking armies that rampaged along the Trent Valley from 865. After rebuilding in monumental style overseen by Bishop Eadnoth, the new church of St Mary was generously endowed by Leofric, Earl of Mercia and his wife Godgifu, better known as Lady Godiva. Their charter dated 1054 grants the Trentside settlements of Newark, Brampton, Marton and Fledborough to the minster along with the manor of Stow itself and income from various other sources. Leofric and Godiva owned other manors along the Trent including Branston and King's Bromley in Staffordshire. Sympathetically restored in the 19th century, the sheer size of St Mary's gives a clue to its former status. Tall walls, a steeply pitched roof and the arches of a spacious crossing echo the Saxon cathedral. Later Norman influences show in the nave and chancel. Although the see was moved

to Lincoln in 1073, a bishop's palace continued to be maintained at Stow Park.

A simple, enchanting eighth-century crypt at Repton somehow survived desecration when a Viking army destroyed the monastery during the winter of 873/4. This was the mausoleum of the Mercian kings. Four columns, each carved from a single block of stone and decorated with a spiral pattern, support a vaulted roof. Sixty years after devastation a church rose from the ruins. Fragments of 10th-century masonry are visible at the east end of St Wystan's today. Incredibly the Saxon crypt remained undiscovered until 1779 when a workman digging a grave in the chancel floor broke through the ceiling and fell into the void.

Under Cnut, who professed himself a Christian, the Church began to re-establish itself. The earlier depredations of Viking attacks had obliterated Anglo-Saxon monasticism in the north and east. When Saxon noble, Wulfric Spot, founded Burton Abbey c.1002, it was for many years, if only by a few feet, the only monastery north of the Trent. A position close

30 *A Saxon doorway and characteristic Norman herringbone masonry preserved at St Peter's Church, Farndon.*

31 *St John the Baptist Church, Armitage was rebuilt in the style of a Norman predecessor in the 19th century. Carved stone masks rescued from an arch of the old building were used to build a novel churchyard cross (inset). Since this picture was taken around 1910, a screen of trees has grown up between the river and the church.*

to a strategically important river crossing and the Island of Andresey, where a chapel sheltering the remains of St Modwen attracted visitors. William the Conqueror himself came to kneel at the shrine on Andresey. Pilgrims were a sound commercial proposition and contributed to making Burton Abbey the wealthiest religious house in Staffordshire.

Around the time of the founding of Burton Abbey, a Saxon church, important enough to be built of stone, was built just four miles upstream near an ancient ford at Walton-on-Trent. Saxon masonry can still be seen in the walls of St Lawrence's Church, Walton and at St Michael's Church, Stanton-by-Bridge. As well as the cross at St John's, Alkborough, fragments of Saxon preaching crosses survive at the churches of St Peter ad Vincula, Stoke-upon-Trent; St Wystan's, Repton; St Peter's, Shelford; and Holy Trinity, Rolleston. St Peter's Church, Farndon has a

Saxon doorway although not in its original position. Saxon foundations lie beneath St Peter's, East Bridgford. A series of decorated friezes and sculpted panels in the church of St Mary and St Hardulph at Breedon on the Hill makes up the finest collection of Anglo-Saxon carvings in the country.

In a land of wooden buildings, stone churches had a practical purpose beyond religion. Towers provided communities with a store, refuge, and lookout point.

In the aftermath of the Norman Conquest, the Council of London (1072) ordered all bishops to organise their sees from fortified towns. Bishop Remigius suppressed the recently re-established monastic house at Stow and transferred his headquarters to Lincoln. Here he laid the foundations of a new cathedral that would be completed in 1092 by his successor, Alexander.

Norman influence, the result of a massive church building programme unrivalled until Victorian times, can be traced in the splendid nave of Southwell Minster and other Trent Valley churches. At Melbourne, a splendidly extravagant 'mini-cathedral' replaced a Saxon church. Characteristic herringbone masonry typical of early-Norman style can be seen at St Mary's, Stow and also in the churches of Knaith, Marton, Littleborough, Averham, Farndon, Rolleston, and Church Laneham. A carved tympanum at Hoveringham shows St Michael fighting dragons, a figurative depiction of the earthly struggle between good and evil. St Clement's Church, Fiskerton is full of Norman fragments, though possibly scavenged from elsewhere. There is Norman work in the lower stages of the church towers at Frodingham, Fledborough and Sutton on Trent. St Mary Magdalene, Newark has massive Norman piers at the crossing and a Norman crypt. St John the Baptist, Collingham has a Norman north arcade. Churches at Littleborough, East Bridgford, Sawley, Twyford, and Stanton-by-Bridge have Norman chancel arches. A fragment of Norman cable moulding surrounds a piscina niche at Wilford. Norman masonry fragments are visible in walls at St Helen's, Burton Joyce; St James's, Swarkestone; and All Saints, King's Bromley.

There are Norman doorways at Bottesford, Attenborough, Long Eaton, Newton Solney, and Alrewas. St John the Baptist, Armitage, its squat tower visible above a fringe of trees on a rocky spur west of the river, was cleverly rebuilt in the style of its Norman predecessor in the 19th century. Carved masks, originally part of a doorway arch, were rescued and used to construct a novel churchyard cross. The village takes its name from a hermitage pre-dating the church. Norman traces were discovered in 1870 during restoration of St Andrew's Church at Weston-on-Trent.

Like rivers in the pre-Christian age, bridges in medieval England had a spiritual dimension. They were a physical representation of the bridge from this world to the next. Travel was a dangerous business. Most bridges displayed a prominent wayside cross. Many had a resident hermit who would say prayers for travellers in return for alms. Before the Reformation, Holme Cross stood beside the landing stage of the ferry to North Muskham.

In the 12th century, the Great Bridge of Burton-on-Trent was among the first in the country to incorporate a bridge chapel, dedicated to St James, patron saint of pilgrims. Other important bridges followed the example. A chapel on Swarkestone Bridge, looked after by priests from

32 The 'Great Bridge' at Burton-on-Trent followed a curving line across three separate arms of the river. A 12th-century bridge chapel, dedicated to St James, was one of the earliest in the country. Bridge chapels dispensed food, comfort and spiritual care in return for alms. The chapel was demolished in 1777 and the bridge replaced in 1864.

Repton Priory, was added in 1249. Nottingham's Hethbethe Bridge had a chapel dedicated to St Mary by 1303. Geoffrey Wolseley endowed a chantry chapel at Wolseley Bridge in the early 1340s. For travellers, bridge chapels offered a place of sanctuary where early morning mass could be attended before setting out to face the hazards of the open road. Bequests to the Church specifically for the building or repair of bridges were common before the Reformation. Gifts were given in return for indulgences and in order that masses would be held to ease the passage of departed souls. One of the religious convictions that characterised the age was a sure and certain expectation of facing purgatory in the afterlife.

William Peveril founded Lenton Priory for the Cluniac order in the 1100s. The monks controlled much of the trade in medieval Nottingham and Lenton became the wealthiest and most powerful monastic house in the Trent Valley. Richard, Earl of Chester set up a small cell of Augustinian monks at Calke c.1115. Ralph de Ayncourt established the Augustinian order at Thurgaton Priory c.1130. Ranulph de Gernon, Earl of Chester, chose Trentham as the site for a priory of Augustinian canons in 1153. His action, probably a desperate attempt at spiritual damage limitation after a violent life, prompted by his impending death. Maud, Countess of Chester established Repton Priory for the Augustinian cell at Calke in 1172, an act of conspicuous piety after poisoning her husband the likely motivation. Around 1170,

Ralph Alselin, lord of the manor of Laxton, founded an Augustinian priory at Shelford.

Augustinian monks were not an enclosed order but worked in the community as priests, celebrating mass, organising schools and running hospitals. The Cistercians, for whom Reynerus Evermue founded a nunnery at Heynings near Lea in the late 12th century, were originally a secluded order who followed an austere code. Knaith Hall and St Mary's Church share a riverside site associated with the nunnery but a lack of hard confirmatory evidence leaves room for doubt. Shallow depressions visible at Hermit Dam, east of Lea, indicate the site of the nunnery fishponds. Many of the endowments included fisheries on the Trent, an important acquisition for members of religious houses who celebrated a number of feast days on which meat was prohibited.

Henry de Audley founded the Cistercian Abbey of Our Lady at Hulton on the banks of the infant Trent in 1219. Within the borough of Nottingham, Henry III gave land to the Franciscans, or Grey Friars, at Broadmarsh and around 1276 Reginald, Lord Grey of Wilton and Sir John Shirley jointly endowed a Carmelite house of White Friars. At Newark, Augustinian monks took over a Franciscan friary in the 15th century. All the religious houses were dissolved at the Reformation and the land was redistributed. The buildings of Repton Priory were being systematically pulled down by Gilbert Thacker to prevent any attempt at reinstatement under Mary Tudor when the

.IIII.

m̄ In LEA. hr̄ Fulcheri 7 II. frs ej. III. car̄ tre 7 dim̄ ad glđ. Ibidē h̄b Vlchil dim̄ car̄ tre ad glđ. Tra ad. V. car̄. Ibi Robt̄ h̄o comitis h̄t nc̄. I. car̄. 7 XVI. uilt 7 II. focħ cū. III. car̄. 7 dimiđ pifcariā de. X. den. 7 I. paffagiū de. XII. den. 7 c. ac̄s p̄ti. 7 c. ac̄s filuæ minutæ. T.R.E. uat. c. fot. m̄ XXX. fot. Tailla. XX. fot.

33 *The Domesday Book entry for Lea records a shared fishery (dimid piscaria) worth 10d. (x den/arii]) and a ferry (passagiu) valued at 12d. (xii den/arii]).*

34 *Mount Pavilion at Colwich, Staffordshire, built in Gothic style by Viscount Tamworth, became St Mary's Abbey in 1836 and continues a long tradition of monasticism in the Trent Valley.*

executors of Sir John Port purchased them in 1557. Under the terms of Port's will, Repton's famous public school was founded on the site. Most visible of a few remaining fragments of the Priory building is a 14th-century gateway arch. Calke had a number of transient owners before Henry Harpur bought the estate. The Harpur family was on the rise from minor gentry to wealthy baronets, largely thanks to a prudent family tradition of marrying rich heiresses. A grand mansion, Calke Abbey, was built in 1703 and remained in the family until Charles Harpur-Crewe died in 1981 and the house became famous as a time capsule of untouched rooms saved for the nation after a vigorous campaign caught the public imagination. Thomas Heneage was granted the land

belonging to Heynings nunnery and the friary in Broadmarsh. The friary site now lies beneath Broadmarsh Shopping Centre. Lenton Priory came to a stickier end than most. In 1538, Prior Nicholas Heath, along with a fellow monk, four labourers and a priest, was hung, drawn and quartered for high treason. The group may have been involved in underground resistance to the Reformation but it is just as likely the charge was trumped up because of a reluctance to co-operate with the Crown Commissioners or surrender priory valuables. Those who admitted various crimes and misdemeanours, true or not, were usually dealt with generously. The prior of Thurgaton confessed to serial adultery and was granted Fiskerton Hall and a yearly pension of £40.

Michael Stanhope leased the valuable estate of Lenton and acquired the manor of Shelford. Sir Edward Aston purchased Hulton Abbey. James Leveson of Wolverhampton acquired the land belonging to Trentham Priory and built Trentham Hall. William Crompton, a London mercer, bought the land of Stone Priory. The remains of the Augustinian friary at Newark were demolished in the 18th century and a house was built on the site. Sir William Paget, a principal secretary of state to Henry VIII, was granted the Benedictine abbey at Burton-on-Trent. Another court insider, William Cooper, acquired the lands of Thurgaton Priory.

A slender thread of continuity kept monasticism in the Trent Valley alive. Hawkesyard Hall at Armitage, built in 1760 and extended by the Spode family of pottery manufacture fame in 1839, was home to Dominican monks for over a century from 1894. It has only recently reverted to secular use as a business complex. In an apt nod to the past, a spa occupying part of the site offers retreats. Gothic style Mount Pavilion at Colwich, built by Viscount Tamworth in 1825, was taken over in 1836 by a convent of Benedictine nuns. The eight-bell carillon of St Mary's Abbey, installed in 1937, is a feature of local life, regulating activity within the abbey and ringing out across the Trent Valley. Local poet Chris McDonnell captured the 6 a.m. peal in 1999: 'Bell-toll and bird-song of a dawn-still morning rings and sings across the tiles of houses blinded still by sleep marking darkness passing'. St Dominic's Convent was established at Stone in 1853. Crusading architect and Roman Catholic convert, A.W.N. Pugin, designed the tiny chapel of St Anne in which the Dominican sisters worship. From 1903 to 1973, when Newark and Sherwood District Council bought it for offices, Kelham Hall was home to an order of Anglican monks, the Society of the Sacred Mission, who used it primarily as a theological college.

Three

Commerce and the Trent Navigation

For the settlements dotted along its banks the River Trent was an important means of transport and communication. Gainsborough and Torksey grew into significant ports for sea-going ships. Shallower draught vessels navigated the upper reaches. Newark and Nottingham both had busy trading wharves.

Early 'flash' locks made use of simple gate weirs to collect a sufficient head of water that could be released to aid the passage of boats through shallows. 'Pound' locks, where gates at each end of a pen operate in tandem allowing water levels within to rise or fall, were introduced into England in the mid-1560s. The first pound lock on the Trent, probably only the second in the country, was constructed by Sir Thomas Stanhope at Shelford in 1576 to control water diverted to drive the wheel of

his corn mill. A series of additional weirs and dams affected flow in the river at Shelford to the extent that legal objections were lodged. Sir Thomas was not a popular man. Neighbours took the opportunity to add a raft of general grievances to the quarrel. A tangle of claims and counter-claims delayed a final ruling. The Chief Justice referred the case to Privy Council. As tempers frayed, frustrated locals took matters into their own hands in 1593 and destroyed the lock. The affair was investigated by Star Chamber and continued to simmer for many years. Not until after the 1699 Trent Navigation Act was the next pound lock built on the Trent, at King's Mills.

Convenient access to the Trent enabled landowners in Staffordshire, Derbyshire, and Nottinghamshire to exploit coal resources

35   *Trade along the Trent from their Nottingham estate at Wollaton was the cornerstone of the Willoughby family fortune and financed the building of Renaissance showpiece Wollaton Hall, designed by Robert Smythson. Nottingham City Council purchased the hall and grounds in 1924.*

on their estates. Most successful was the Willoughby family of Wollaton. Between 1580 and 1588, Sir Francis Willoughby built Wollaton Hall out of the profits. The Willoughby's had their own fleet of open barges or 'lighters' and distribution warehouses at Gainsborough. Coal was delivered to Southwell, Newark, Retford and Torksey for onward carriage to Lincoln, Boston and Grantham. Barges returned with food and consumer items brought in by coasters from London for sale at Lenton Fair. By the 1600s, a prototype railway employing horses to pull open waggons along wooden tracks connected pits at Wollaton to the river. As the number of coalfields grew, timber for pit props shipped from the Baltic ports became a regular return cargo.

Beer brewed at Burton-on-Trent using mineral-rich local well water filtered through beds of gypsum began to build a reputation for exceptional quality. An advertisement in the *Spectator* magazine of 1712 announced the availability in London of 'Genuine Burton ale brewed to the greatest perfection for keeping by sea or land'. Casks of ale were shipped along the Trent via Stockwith, Gainsborough and Hull to meet a growing market in the capital. Demand ensured that premium prices could be charged to compensate for delivery costs.

Road carriers and shipping merchants were in direct competition. River transport offered bulk carriage at a third of the cost and, although seasonal flooding and dry spells were a persistent problem, it was generally reliable. Roads, a mainly parochial responsibility, were poorly maintained and deeply rutted. Many routes in winter months became impassable for days at a time. Pack-horse trains criss-crossed the country but ponies were limited by the capacity of panniers slung either side and to loads of around two and a half cwt.

Conflicts of interest intensified as traffic on the river increased. Fords in use from ancient times and essential for overland routes were dangerous shallows for heavily laden boats. Weirs and dams controlling mill sluices, or operating as fish traps, caused obstruction and interfered with water levels. Sailing barges had to be 'haled' through shallows and strong adverse currents by teams of men on the riverbank hauling on ropes attached to vessels' bows. A practice opposed by many of the landed gentry who objected to having their riparian estates crossed by gangs of men generally considered ruffians.

36 Cordale *passing West Stockwith, heading upriver with the tide.*

37 *Former warehouse buildings beside the Trent at Shardlow now converted as dwellings.*

Economics dictated progress. Trade along the Trent, both domestically and overseas, particularly with the Baltic countries, was increasing. Various plans were put forward to improve the Navigation. The brewers of Burton-on-Trent, ironware manufacturers in the Black Country, salt merchants in Staffordshire and Cheshire, and rural cheese factors in the north Midlands, all wanted better access to an inland port for their products.

At the beginning of the 17th century, Nottingham had for many years been the natural head of Navigation. Shallows and rapids between Sawley and Wilford deterred development further upstream. Goods from Derbyshire and beyond were carried overland to wharves below Nottingham's Trent Bridge.

Despite opposition from the vested interests of Nottingham, Leonard Fosbrooke, lessee of the ferry at Wilden, a busy river crossing south of Shardlow, extended the Navigation inland.

It was a tough business. Boat owners and merchants conspired to land goods illegally in order to avoid paying tolls. Fosbrooke policed the river relentlessly and ruthlessly to protect his trade. Under his management Shardlow became a thriving port. Success enabled Fosbrooke to build Shardlow Hall in 1684.

Plans to make the river navigable to Burton-on-Trent, proposed by local lord of the manor William, 6th Baron Paget, were approved by Act of Parliament in 1699, subject to private finance being raised to cover the cost. A quay and warehouse opened at Willington, prompting a threat by Nottingham Corporation to block the arches of Trent Bridge with chains and charge a toll for boats to pass. At Shardlow, the Fosbrooke family employed fair means and foul to frustrate progress. After a decade in which no further headway was made, Lord Paget sublet the shipping rights to a Derbyshire businessman, George Hayne. The deal included property

38 *Fiskerton Wharf was one of many tranship- ment points where boats bound upriver lightened their loads when water levels were low.*

formerly part of Burton Abbey and land at the Soho, an area beside an arm of the river called the Fleet. Hayne took over in 1711 and managed to negotiate a mutually beneficial deal with Fosbrooke, who the year before had concluded an arrangement with a group of 58 London merchants that ensured a virtual monopoly of the lucrative trade in cheese. A wharf built on the Soho opened for business in 1712. The original proposal put before Parliament included plans to dredge the shallows between Shardlow and Burton-on-Trent, straighten various meanders and cut new channels. In the event, little initial investment was made beyond the construction of locks at Winshill and King's Mills. At these particularly shallow points it was necessary to co-ordinate the opening of mill sluices to ensure sufficient depth of water. Single-masted ketches operating on the upper river were capable of handling a payload of 40 tons. Under the dif- ficult conditions, cargoes were restricted to less, often not much more than 12 tons. Occasionally boats had to offload part of their cargo to pass through shallows, unloading again downstream and backtracking relay-fashion to pick up goods

left behind. Burton's long, curving medieval stone bridge with 36 low-slung arches was a further hazard to be negotiated. Despite these problems the venture was a success. Depend- ing on river conditions, boats made the return trip from Burton-on-Trent to Gainsborough in eight to 12 days. A single square sail was hoisted in favourable winds. Muscle power was applied to pole or hale against the current and through shallows. By 1750, some two hundred boats regularly made use of the new facilities and Burton's Soho Wharf was handling seven thousand tons of freight annually. Keen to secure return cargoes, ship owners operating out of the Baltic ports into Hull actively sought custom- ers in Eastern Europe for Burton-on-Trent's increasingly renowned ale. Payment in kind was a common arrangement. Pig iron, hemp, timber and other imported goods supplied forge mills, ropewalks, cooperages and a range of other businesses. Significant inward investment was attracted and the town enjoyed a burst of economic growth. Men such as brewer Samuel Sketchley of Newark moved to Burton-on-Trent in 1740 to take advantage of the brand.

When the lease came up for renewal in 1762, the port at Burton-on-Trent could look back on 50 successful years. Continuing prosperity, however, was threatened by proposals for a cross-country canal linking the navigable reaches of the rivers Trent and Mersey. Josiah Wedgwood was among a number of influential businessmen and landowners actively promoting the scheme. The support of Earl Gower, Lord Lieutenant of Staffordshire, and George Anson of Shugborough Hall was enlisted. Wedgwood had established his own pottery business at Burslem in 1759 after learning the trade as an apprentice in the family business. An instinctive flair for business combined with high-quality products brought rapid success. Wedgwood acquired influential and high profile customers. By 1765, thanks to the patronage of Queen Charlotte, he was able to style himself 'Potter to Her Majesty'. Water transport was the most efficient way of delivering his classically inspired earthenware to a growing market but entailed an overland journey to the nearest inland port. Fragile pottery was packed in bracken, crated and carried 30 miles to Willington Wharf for onward despatch along the Trent. Flint from eastern counties was shipped back. Burnt and ground to a powder, flint was added to ball clay from Devon, Dorset and Cornwall to strengthen and whiten the mix.

In 1761, gifted engineer James Brindley showed what was possible by building what was effectively England's first canal, a channel connecting the Duke of Bridgewater's coalmines at Worsley to the River Mersey at Runcorn. With the Industrial Revolution gaining momentum, factory-based mass production was replacing small-scale cottage industries. Britain's growing empire was a huge untapped market. Steam engines were superseding waterpower and driving up demand for coal and iron. Along the Trent and its tributaries, corn and fulling mills were converted as furnaces for smelting and forging, or as flint and colour mills for the pottery industry. An antiquated transport system was creaking under the strain.

With support from Wedgwood and others, Brindley drew up plans for an artificial waterway or 'Grand Trunk', from Preston Brook in Cheshire to join the Trent Navigation, envisaged as the first stage in establishing cross country links between the ports of Hull, London, Bristol, Liverpool and Manchester.

It was against the background of these proposals that negotiations for renewal of the port lease at Burton-on-Trent were conducted. Sir William Paget's grandson, now ennobled as the Earl of Uxbridge, set the price at £4,000. John Hayne, who had taken over the family business from his uncle George, offered a sum of £3,000 subject to a clawback provision if the proposed Grand Trunk was built within 10 years. A group of leading local businessmen, including the Earl's representative William Wyatt, put together an alternative bid valuing the lease at £2,500 but with no qualifying clauses. This group, constituted as the Burton Boat Company, took over the lease.

An enabling Act was passed by Parliament in 1766 allowing work to start on what would become the Trent and Mersey Canal. Josiah Wedgwood ceremonially dug the first spade of earth. His plans for a new pottery factory and village to be called Etruria, alongside the route, were already at an advanced stage. The canal was the most ambitious civil engineering project ever attempted in this country. Seventy-six locks, 213 road bridges and 160 aqueducts were necessary. With limited resources, Brindley

39 *Men working in pairs used wharfingers' scissors attached to a wooden yoke to lift and move heavy freight.*

tackled problems with resourcefulness, logic and simplicity. For most of its 93-mile journey the route follows the contours of the Trent Valley. At Alrewas, canal and river unite in an ingeniously expedient 250-yard level crossing.

Burton Boat Company tried to persuade Brindley to terminate the canal at their wharf. For both practical and commercial reasons the offer was rejected. Brindley was keen to avoid the shoals that caused problems in the upper reaches of the Navigation and as far as possible to usurp the Boat Company's business. In a calculated move he chose to make the connection to the Trent 19 miles downriver of Burton-on-Trent at Shardlow. Burton Boat Company dug a cutting direct from their wharf to the new canal with the intention of allowing boats easy access to both waterways. Brindley's response was to ensure a channel wide enough to accommodate broad-beamed river craft only as far as Horninglow on the outskirts of Burton-on-Trent. Here, still one mile short of the Boat Company's proposed link, moorings and warehousing were built around a terminal basin. Further inland the new canal was only accessible to narrowboats. Connection of the

river cutting was then refused on technical grounds. By the time locks had been installed to counter a drop of over three feet between canal and river and the link was finally made, the Trent and Mersey Canal had been fully open for 17 years. Although the river port continued to operate into the 19th century, carriage lost to the canal led to an irreversible decline.

The opening of the Trent and Mersey Canal turned rural Shardlow into a booming Georgian town at the hub of a countrywide waterway network. From a single warehouse the port grew rapidly. Further stores and wharves were added. There was stabling for around two hundred horses. Boatbuilders supplied carriers on the Trent with broad-beamed riverboats and canal companies with narrowboats. Boat owners James Sutton (Cavendish Boat Company) and Soresby and Flack among others operated light, fast flyboats.

A scheme proposed by Newark Navigation Commissioners to make a branch of the Trent, into which the River Devon flowed, navigable at Newark was delayed by Nottingham's business community, exercising rights on the river first granted in the 12th century. In 1772, Parliament

40 *Innovative engineer James Brindley built the Trent and Mersey Canal following the contours of the Trent Valley. River and canal briefly merge in an ingenious 'level crossing' at Alrewas where a long towpath bridge spans the Trent.*

41 *A horse on Long Horse Bridge tows a narrowboat loaded with carboys from the Trent and Mersey Canal into the River Trent at Derwent Mouth near Shardlow. 'Water Bridge', in the background, was built to carry Long Eaton's water supply in 1909, shortly before this photograph was taken.*

42 *Sailing barges and Upper Trent craft moored at Huddlestones Wharf, Newark Basin, c.1900.*

overturned objections and Newark Dyke was cut the following year, replacing the channel via Averham, Kelham and South Muskham. Two weirs increased the flow of water and, with the addition of Newark Nether or 'Bottom' Lock and Newark Town or 'Top' Lock, a direct route through the town was created with an accompanying towpath. A sharp angle at the entrance to Nether Lock required caution. Approaching craft were hidden from view and the weir stream exerted a pull on turning boats.

With improvements in place port business at Newark boomed. At its peak in the early 19th century, wharfingers were handling over fifty thousand tons of cargo annually, much of it coal. Newark, already an established malting centre, was fast gaining a reputation for brewing beer. Samuel Sketchley junior reversed his father's move to Burton-on-Trent and returned to lease Town Wharf Brewery in 1766. With his partner William Handley, Sketchley expanded production and, making full use of the new facilities for shipping, built a thriving trade with

43 *A canal link known familiarly as 'Cuckoo Dyke' from Chesterfield to the Trent at West Stockwith opened in 1777. The tidal lock requires a careful approach from boats.*

44 *A busy scene at the Trent Navigation Company warehouse, Newark, around 1900 shows goods being transferred to Upper Trent craft for onward shipment upriver.*

Russia and the Baltic States. Other breweries followed his example, all located along the river for easy access to a wharf.

Between 1769 and 1777 a 46-mile canal from Chesterfield to a tidal lock at West Stockwith Basin was constructed. Trent craft were able to navigate the new canal as far as Retford, consigning a well used but difficult route, along the River Idle from Bawtry, to decline. Narrowboats on the Chesterfield Canal were of an individual design. Cabins barely protruded above the gunwales, a design feature dictated by restricted headroom in Norwood tunnel, and bulky wooden fenders were wrapped around bow and stern. These distinctive vessels became familiarly known as 'Cuckoos' and the canal as 'Cuckoo Dyke'. A variety of cargoes including coal, stone, timber, bricks, lead, iron and grain were carried. Stone to build the Houses of Parliament travelled along the Chesterfield Canal to West Stockwith where it was transferred to Humber sloops bound for Westminster. An occasional cargo was silt or 'warp', dug from the banks of the Trent. This was dried at Walkeringham and the powder sold for use as commercial silver polish.

The success of the Trent and Mersey and Chesterfield canals triggered a spate of parallel developments. An Act of 1776 enabled the River Soar to be made navigable from the Trent to Loughborough. Spurs were added into the mining villages of North West Leicestershire and Rutland, and to Market Harborough in Leicestershire. By 1779, the Erewash Canal linked coalfields in Derbyshire to the Trent at Sawley.

Pilferage, rife on the river, was a considerable problem. Two men convicted of stealing pottery from a warehouse at Willington Wharf were sentenced to seven years' transportation. An allegedly fierce dog brought in to guard the warehouse was itself stolen. Much petty theft went undetected. A few hanks of silk could be pulled from a bale almost unnoticeably. Rounds of cheese were easily spirited away. Sugar was taken from sacks and replaced with sand. A single iron hoop could be loosened from a cask of ale, holes pierced and a quantity of beer siphoned off before topping up the barrel with water, plugging the holes and refitting the hoop to cover up evidence of tampering. The proprietors of the Trent and Mersey Canal attempted to counter the problem by putting responsibility for goods carried firmly with boat owners. A refundable bond was levied against which any losses could be charged.

William Jessop (1745-1814), born in Devon, learned much of his engineering and surveying skills at Newark and became an adopted son, living in Appleton Gate from 1784 to 1805 and serving two terms of office as mayor. In 1782, Jessop and a fellow engineer, Robert Whitworth, were engaged to survey the river from Shardlow to Gainsborough. Their findings and Jessop's subsequent recommendations laid the foundations for a raft of improvements that took place towards the close of the 18th century.

An Act of 1783 placed the whole of the Navigation from Shardlow to Gainsborough, apart from the new cutting through Newark that was owned by Newark Navigation Commission, in the hands of the Company of Proprietors of the Trent Navigation who appointed William Jessop company engineer. The Trent Navigation Company, as it became, remained in charge until nationalisation in 1948, first under the Docks & Inland Waterways Executive, a division of the British Transport Commission, and from 1962 British Waterways. Below Gainsborough, Associated British Ports succeeded the Humber Conservancy Council and British Transport Docks Board in 1983 as the responsible authority.

Nottingham Corporation had managed to win a concession from Parliament in 1726 to allow limited use of horses to tow boats, but it was not until 1783 that hauling with horses instead of men was more generally allowed. Two horses could do the work of a dozen men at less than a quarter of the cost. Strips of land were rented from landowners and within two years a 68-mile riverside towpath from Shardlow to Gainsborough was complete, allowing horse-drawn narrowboats to use the river and removing the need for freight to be transferred to sailing barges. Roving points were established where the towing path switched banks. Horses were ferried across on a sunken deck. When winds, currents and tides were favourable, horses travelled on board. Untended draught horses feeding from containers draped around their muzzles outside local hostelries were such a common sight in Sawley that villagers were nicknamed 'nosebaggers'.

Between 1789 and 1792, Nottingham Canal was constructed from the Erewash Canal to the river below Trent Bridge. An extension to Langley Mill joined the Cromford Canal. Beeston Canal (1795) completed a link from the Nottingham Canal, bypassing shallows at Wilford and sidelining Nottingham Wharf, where a capstan had proved necessary to help boats through the tricky river passage at Trent Bridge.

45 *A cutting at Sawley, dug to by-pass shallows in 1795, is now the busiest stretch of the river. An adjacent marina occupying former aggregate quarries is among the largest in Europe.*

46 *Trentside Keadby around 1890, downstream of the wooden jetty and the entrance to the Stainforth and Keadby Canal.*

Side cuts at Sawley (1795) and Cranfleet (1797) either side of Trent Lock ended continual dredging using a horse-drawn gravel plough and removed the need for winching boats through shallows (all boats were fitted with a winch at the bow). Shoals at Holme Pierrepont were by-passed in 1800. In the early years of the 19th century, the Roman causeway at Littleborough was removed, fords were scoured to a minimum depth of 24 inches, and a number of new weirs and locks built.

In 1796, the Derby Canal opened, connecting Sandiacre and the Erewash Canal to Swarkestone. To protect their investment, Derby

Canal Company bought the shipping rights on the River Derwent and immediately closed this rather unreliable route to the Trent. Within months there was a cut from the River Soar at Loughborough to Leicester. Grantham Canal, locking into the Trent at West Bridgford, followed. A safety hawser between the Grantham and Nottingham Canals prevented narrowboats crossing the river below Trent Bridge being caught broadside in the current and swept downstream. By the 1840s, Navigation Bridge had been built, allowing boats to be towed between the canals, but after sustaining flood damage in 1875 it was demolished.

The Stainforth and Keadby Canal, part of the Sheffield and South Yorkshire Navigation, supplanted a difficult navigation on the River Don in 1802.

The completion by 1805 of canal links from the Midlands to London through Coventry and Oxford significantly reduced the amount of freight shipped via Hull and effectively ended the Navigation above Shardlow. Heavy tariffs introduced by Russia to restrict imports and promote domestic industry disrupted the lucra-

tive Baltic trade. War with France left ports blockaded. Despite these setbacks, the last quarter of the 18th century and the early part of the 19th witnessed the heyday of traffic on the River Trent. Investors in the Trent Navigation Company made hefty profits. New markets emerged as the British Empire expanded. India Pale Ale, a new slightly sparkling beer suitable for hot climates and able to withstand being transported over long distances, became a major export.

Boatwrights struggled to keep pace with demand. Shallow draught vessels of 14½-ft beam were specifically designed for the upper river. Larger Humber keels and Humber sloops with a beam of 15½ ft were built at Stockwith, Beckingham and Gainsborough. The Humber keel with its flat bottom, single central mast and large square-rigged mainsail has a lineage that many imagine can be traced back through medieval vessels to the Viking longship. Loaded to the gunwales they could carry up to one hundred tons in roomy holds and required a draught of one fathom (six feet). Keels were built with a beam to suit inland waterway

47   *A steel-hulled Humber sloop passing Watson's Boatyard at Gainsborough. A fore and aft gaff-rigged mainsail coupled with a small headsail enabled the vessel to sail close hauled to windward. Sloops were graceful under sail and performed well in the tricky tidal currents of the Humber.*

48 *Gainsborough United Steam Packet Company's paddle steamer* Scarborough. *Packet boats ran regular passenger and small parcel services between Gainsborough and Hull until the First World War.*

lock sizes on the Trent, and Sheffield size for the canalised rivers of South Yorkshire. On the Trent Navigation the keel excelled. Sailing close-hauled into the wind a topsail was hoisted to extend the leading edge of the mainsail. A leeboard lowered over the side amidships controlled drift. Humber sloops shared the same hull as the Humber keel but had a fore and aft gaff-rigged mainsail, a small headsail and the mast and leeboard were set further forward, one-third of the distance from the bow. Sloops were graceful sailing vessels, ideal at handling tidal seaways. Blunt, rounded bows and sturdy build coped well with the choppy swell and tricky cross currents of the Humber Estuary. Inland, the boom of the fore and aft rig was unwieldy, often swinging out over the riverbank where it could be fouled.

By the middle of the 19th century, timber began to be replaced as the material of choice for hulls. The first all-steel barge was built for the Tomlinson shipping company by Watson's of Beckingham. Under Captain Thomas Taylor-Chapman, *Trent 1* worked primarily between Lincoln and Hull. The vessel turned out longer than planned and its rudder had to be folded at right angles in order to fit within locks. *Trent 2*, also built for Tomlinson's with Tom

Taylor-Chapman's son Joseph Chapman as master, and subsequent vessels were six feet shorter. Generations of the Chapman family have been involved with the Trent Navigation. It was Joseph Chapman, then in charge of the powered barge *Kestrel*, who with his mate famously managed to rope a whale that had strayed into the Trent and towed it to Gainsborough.

Pioneering engineer Richard Trevithick built the first steam driven carriage in 1801. A few years later he adapted one of his engines to power a barge. Trevithick's innovative ideas encouraged further development. Steam-powered boats began work on the river in 1814. The advent of powered vessels reduced the 56-mile journey from Gainsborough to Hull from two or three days to a mere five hours.

Packet boats were soon offering passengers an alternative to uncomfortable road journeys by stagecoach. From Nottingham to Cromford and Leicester a choice of first- or second-class travel was available. By the 1820s, a regular service between Gainsborough and Nottingham was established with connections to Bawtry, Lincoln and elsewhere. In the 1830s, sailing ships left Gainsborough for Hull twice weekly and steamers ran daily. A service between Gainsborough and London was introduced. The return journey took 36 hours and cost 4s 9d. Competition between the Gainsborough United Steam Packet Company, the River Trent Packet Company of Nottingham and rival companies on the Humber led to good deals for passengers who often travelled free. Steamers continued to run until the First World War.

For a time, Gainsborough was the busiest inland port in Britain. Trade in the town thrived. The steam packets made the town's market accessible to a scattered rural population. A Customs Office was set up and in 1841 Gainsborough achieved full port status, allowing foreign vessels and imported goods to bypass the bonded warehouses at Hull.

The upper river was still subject to unpredictable delays. Dry summers increased the risk of grounding. Ice could close the Navigation for weeks at a time in severe winter snaps. Increased silting and dangers posed by wrecks were a problem in the lower reaches. As the 19th century

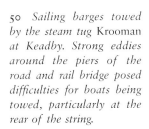

49 *Icy conditions at Gainsborough when the river froze in the harsh winter of 1946/7. Unpredictable delays due to adverse weather conditions were a feature of the Trent Navigation.*

50 *Sailing barges towed by the steam tug* Krooman *at Keadby. Strong eddies around the piers of the road and rail bridge posed difficulties for boats being towed, particularly at the rear of the string.*

progressed, the railways took more and more traffic from the waterways. Water transport was cheaper than rail but slower and increasingly it was the railway companies that were in control. Ambergate Railway Company purchased the Grantham Canal in 1854 and added Nottingham Canal to their portfolio in 1855. Customs and Excise receipts at Gainsborough illustrate the decline. A total in excess of £73,000 collected in 1844 had fallen to little more than £2,000 by 1879. Gainsborough's days as an independent port authority ended in 1881.

In 1887, the Trent Navigation Company decided on direct intervention. From their headquarters on Wilford Street, Nottingham, and with Furley and Company of Gainsborough acting as agents, they began operating their own fleet of vessels. Instead of boats being run literally as small family businesses with a boatman, wife and children living aboard and

51 *By the 1900s, when this family was photographed aboard a sailing barge moored in the Fossdyke, it was more usual for two-man crews to be employed.*

all contributing to the work as remained the case on much of the canal network, it became more usual on the river for all-male crews to be employed.

Steam tugs were capable of towing three or four unpowered 'dumb' craft, either in line or in a V-formation, with a total carrying capacity exceeding four hundred tons. Strong currents were a potential problem for craft under tow at the rear of the string. Swirling eddies around the piers of Keadby Bridge were a particular hazard. Commercial viability depended upon completing improvements that would allow the passage of larger vessels. In 1906, the Trent Navigation Company began dredging a central channel to a consistent depth of one fathom. When the First World War disrupted progress, Nottingham Corporation took over the lease as far as Newark to push ahead with the urgently needed work. A temporary shortage of manpower during wartime brought wives and daughters, some as young as 12 years of age, back to work on family boats.

A new lock at Cromwell, built in 1911, required a series of extensions and modifications to keep pace with the needs of deeper-draught boats. Larger capacity locks with weirs to raise water levels followed at Holme Pierrepont (1922), Stoke Bardolph (1923), Gunthorpe (1925) and Hazelford (1926). Newark Nether Lock was reconstructed. With the need to tranship goods to smaller Upper Trent vessels at Newark removed, journey time between Hull and Nottingham was cut to 24 hours.

The decline in trade was temporarily reversed. Railway sidings were built alongside wharves. Leading oil companies, including Esso, Fina, Regent and Shell, had their own jetties when Colwick Depot opened in 1933. Oil terminals followed at Newark, Althorpe, and Torksey. Lysaghts of Scunthorpe opened a wharf at Flixborough in 1939 with a direct rail link to their steelworks. Flixborough Shipping Company was formed to deliver coal and iron ore to Lysaght's Wharf and collect finished steel. Gainsborough Shipping Company began

52   *Flixborough Wharf, connected by a direct rail link to steelworks at Scunthorpe.*

operating from Watson's former ship building yard at Beckingham. Carriage of sand and gravel contributed to the resurgence. The Trent Valley is one of the main areas for aggregate extraction in England. In the 1920s and '30s, Lincoln and Hull Water Transport built up a large fleet of steam-driven 'gravellers', later converted to diesel. Keels and sloops were fitted with engines or became dumb craft. The last sailing vessels disappeared in the 1940s. Leeboards were removed, making craft more difficult to handle. Masts, useful for lifting when rigged up as cranes with the boom acting as a makeshift derrick, were usually retained after conversion. In 1976, the former sailing keel *Comrade*, withdrawn from commercial service as a powered vessel two years earlier, was restored by the Humber Keel and Sloop Preservation Society and converted back to sail.

Competition kept prices low and reduced profit margins. Much needed resources had to wait until nationalisation of the waterways in 1948. Under Government guidelines 'Scope for commercial development' was recognised. The Trent was given a 'Priority river' categorisation and received public funding for key projects. In

the 1950s, a cut at Holme Pierrepont straightened out a looping meander and enabled a flood lock to be removed. Capacity at Cromwell Lock was increased. Town Lock, Newark was rebuilt. All locks were converted to mechanical operation. A new fleet of powered barges was commissioned. Warehousing in Nottingham was expanded and a container service to European destinations introduced.

Initially, the investment paid off. Larger locks saved time by allowing four-barge strings to pass at a single penning. The largest, at Cromwell, could accommodate eight craft. Although commercial traffic above Nottingham ceased by 1963, carriage between Nottingham and the Humber continued. Road haulage filled the gaps left when a programme of railway rationalisation, begun in the late 1950s, resulted in the closure of wharf sidings. With the aid of tugs fitted with powerful marine diesel engines, sea-going vessels could reach Nottingham. By the 1980s, vessels up to 150 feet in length were operating above Cromwell but competition from road and rail was proving too strong. Oil pipelines replaced river tankers. Deliveries to the petroleum depot at Colwick ended in

53   Humber Trader *passing through Town Lock, Newark heading upriver.*

1971. Government investment in the waterways diminished. Long-term viability, particularly on the upper reaches of the river, was deemed unsustainable. In 1988, British Waterways sold what remained of their fleet. Canal traffic suffered a similar decline. A grant to renovate Colwick oil terminal offered a brief glimmer of hope in 1991 but insufficient business was generated.

For four centuries, coal from the East Midlands pits was among the most important commodities carried on the river. The bulk of supplies for the power stations built along the Trent Valley was delivered by rail. Closure of local collieries resulted in increased imports of foreign coal. Humber International Terminal, the only deep-water multi-purpose port facility between the Thames and the Tees, opened in

2000. Coal imported here is now once more shipped upriver and, with British Waterways actively promoting freight carrying, barges remain a regular sight on the Trent. Commercial traffic is now concentrated on the tidal reaches below Cromwell and the non-tidal Navigation is predominantly, though not exclusively, used by leisure craft.

Components for a gas-fired power station at Staythorpe are due to be delivered by barge. In May 2004, the newly launched multi-purpose pontoon *Terra Marique* delivered a transformer to Cottam Power Station. At 260 feet in length and with a beam of 54 feet, it was the largest vessel ever to pass along the river. Under tow from two tugs the giant sea-going barge was guided upriver, brushing beneath the central arch of Gainsborough's Trent Bridge.

Four

From Quiet Homes and First Beginning:
The Potteries and Rural Staffordshire

High on the windswept moors of north Staffordshire where the source waters of the Trent collect, legend tells of distinctively dark-featured locals descended from Saracens. The major landowner in the 12th century, Bertram de Verdun raised a force to fight in the crusades of Richard Coeur de Lion. Verdun died in the Holy Land but it is possible that a group of captives were brought back to the area by Ormus de Guidon, one of Verdun's tenants. An alternative theory holds that they are the remnant of an ancient British tribal bloodline. Certainly people have lived here from prehistoric times when the springs that emerge would have attracted

reverence. If it were ever true that people here were recognisably different it is no longer. The defining characteristic today is the easy, unforced friendliness typical of people in the Staffordshire Moorlands. Biddulph derives from 'by delf' meaning by the diggings, a reference to coal mining that began in the area a thousand or so years ago. Modern houses enclosing a nucleus of stone cottages mark the recent growth of Biddulph Moor from rural hamlet to medium-sized village. From this roost on the western rim of craggy moorland heights, views of the wide Cheshire plain spread like a rolled out map to the horizon – a patchwork landscape of

54 *Trent Head Well on the edge of Biddulph Moor, official source of the River Trent. Steps inside a small gated enclosure lead to a pipe from which a trickle of water emerges. A brick surround was added in 1935.*

55   *Biddulph Moor to Milton.*

towns and fields with the gleaming white sphere of Jodrell Bank radio telescope in the middle distance. Trent Head Well, official source of the River Trent, is sunk into the muddy edge of a field at the village fringe. In 1996, Staffordshire Moorlands District Council marked the site with a small enclosure. A gate leads to steps cut into squelching earth. At the foot, a pipe is set low into a brick backdrop inscribed 1935, from which a steady dribble of water emerges to seep away along a sedge-squeezed gully. An unprepossessing spot is made special by knowledge of its significance as the birthplace of a mighty waterway, beginning a thread that will be woven into the life of communities from here to the sea. How long before this trickle will merge in the swelling, rolling waters of the Humber Estuary? I had planned to take a sip at the spring but content myself with sprinkling a few drops over my head in symbolic homage.

No more than one of a number of streams, the newborn rivulet tumbles briskly south from Biddulph Moor along Foxlow Hollow, through Crowborough Wood to Knypersley Country Park. From Knypersley Reservoir, a former millpond that was enlarged to feed the Cauldon Canal, the stream officially becomes known as the Head of Trent. Passing between Brown Edge and Ball Green the head stream enters the City of Stoke-on-Trent at Norton Green, collects Ford Green Brook at Milton and formally becomes the River Trent.

Through the Potteries, as the six towns of Tunstall, Burslem, Hanley, Stoke-upon-Trent, Fenton and Longton became collectively known in the second half of the 18th century, the secretive adolescent stream, shallow and barely five yards at its widest, is almost hidden. Through Milton, by Carmountside and into Abbey Hulton, it winds in a cleft sandwiched between Leek Road and the Cauldon Canal. Crossing under the Leek Road to skirt Bucknall Park and Finney Gardens the river ducks below the A52 carriageway and dives under the disused railway line beside the crumbling platform of Bucknall's former station to meet Causeley Brook. Behind

56 *The adolescent Trent is almost hidden as it journeys through the Potteries conurbation between Abbey Hulton and Bucknall.*

57 *The narrow river rushes anonymously behind Leek Road, Bucknall as it approaches Joiner's Square.*

58 *Square-stemmed St John's Wort with its distinctive multi-stamened yellow flowers is well suited to a damp, grassy wetland environment.*

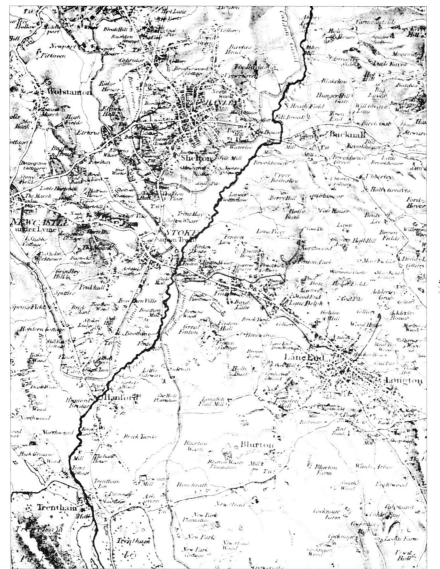

59   *The Potteries to Trentham.*

the retail units and warehouses lining Leek Road the river is an anonymous, fugitive presence, banks unkempt and overgrown. Trent Mill Road and Old Wharf Place are simply suggestive echoes lined with modern houses. An attempt at landscaping on the approach to Joiner's Square has been overtaken by neglect. Culverts carry the flow in concrete tunnels beneath interchanges as the river accompanies Queensway to Hanford, gathering the waters of Fowlea Brook, Chitlings Brook, Lyme Brook and Longton Brook.

The young Trent is not particularly impressive. Easy to understand how the city that bears its name overlooked it for so long. And yet even where past neglect is most obvious, on scrubby banks choked with common bombsite plants such as mugwort and rosebay willowherb, clumps of bird's foot trefoil and square-stemmed St John's Wort can also be found. Knapweed thrives in the damp ground. Spiky globes of teasel stand tall. Minnow shoals dart in the stream, their silver flicker attracting heron and kingfisher.

Ancient bridges near Abbey Farm at Abbey Hulton, Boothen, Hanford, Long Bridge at Trentham, Strongford Bridge and Tittensor have all been replaced in modern times. In the last quarter of the 20th century, a tidal wave of industrial change transformed the Potteries. Unthinkable a decade before it happened, rows of smoking slope-shouldered bottle kilns that had dominated and defined the skyline for centuries vanished. Shelton Iron and Steel Works and the collieries, around which whole communities were built, closed. The National Garden Festival of 1986 instigated the regeneration of Shelton Bar as Festival Park, a leisure and business complex, and set the scene for the 'new look' Potteries. Since then Stoke-on-Trent has woken up to the importance of its unobtrusive asset. A strategy document was published in March 1999 covering the Trent and its Potteries tributaries with the aim of creating a wildlife-friendly network of green spaces. The Rivers of Renewal Project drawn up by Stoke-on-Trent City Council in partnership with The Environment Agency and Severn Trent Water has published a vision intended to direct 'The rediscovery, protection and regeneration of the City's river corridors'. Signs that the river is being cared for and made accessible to people are already apparent throughout the City. Key sites,

including the rich but sensitive environment of Heakley Marshes just inside the City's northern limits where the Cauldon Canal crosses the headwater, have been identified and practical steps taken to safeguard and enhance natural habitat. Waterside Park between Birches Head Road and Cromer Road has opened up a stretch of river that can be enjoyed from a terrace path cut into the slope between the Cauldon Canal and the wriggling, energetic river in the valley bottom. A footpath and cycleway at Sideway leads from Stoke City's former Victoria Football Ground to Hanford Bridge, crossing the river by the new Michelin Bridge. Completed in 2002, it is the first section in a planned River Trent Path through the City.

River pollution reached danger levels as the population grew rapidly throughout the 19th century – an additional health risk for people already exposed to countless smoke-belching kilns, the perils of chlorine gas (a by product of salt glazing carried out to give pots a glossy finish), and an assortment of powdered minerals and chemicals used in the ceramics industry.

Immediately downstream, Trentham was described in 1867 as the 'Cesspool of the Potteries'. With the combined effluent of the conurbation running by his doorstep at Trentham Hall, the Duke of Sutherland provided land nearby for

60   *Trentham Hall, demolished in 1912, was home to the Dukes of Sutherland from the 16th century. The Trent ran through the estate and close to the grand house. Heavy pollution of the river by sewage and industrial effluent from the Potteries conurbation was cited as an influencing factor in the Leveson-Gower family's move away from Trentham.*

61   *The parish church of St Peter ad Vincula, Stoke-upon-Trent occupies a site sacred since at least the seventh century close to where the Trent collects Fowlea Brook. The present church was consecrated in 1830. Masonry from an arch of the earlier, mainly 13th-century building is conserved in the churchyard.*

sewage works. Efforts to improve sanitation were hampered by administrative fragmentation until the formation of the County Borough of Stoke-on-Trent brought local authority unification in 1910. By then the Leveson-Gowers had moved. Trentham Hall was offered to the new Corporation. When they declined it was demolished, and the 750-acre grounds were developed as leisure gardens with Sir Charles Barry's Italian Gardens, laid out in the 1830s, as the main attraction. A ballroom added in the 1920s became a popular music venue. *The Beatles* performed here in 1963. When the Sutherland family sold the estate in 1980, a period of gentle decline followed. Now Trentham Gardens is the focus of a multi-million pound commercial and historic regeneration project. Phase one of the ongoing development with a new bridge across the river re-opened to the public in 2003. In addition to a garden centre and retail village, lake, woodland and heath habitats are being managed for wildlife conservation. A large heronry on an island in Trentham Lake has a population of over forty breeding pairs. The remnants of a herd of fallow deer first brought to the park in 1735 are thriving. There are also outdoor activity facilities.

The County Borough of Stoke-on-Trent was extended in 1922 and became a city in 1925. Stoke-upon-Trent itself was at the heart of an extensive parish centred on the church of St Peter ad Vincula, occupying a long-sacred site at the confluence of the Trent and Fowlea Brook. A mainly 13th-century structure in a poor state of repair was demolished after the new St Peter's Church, built alongside, was consecrated in 1830. Masonry from an arch of the earlier building, discovered during demolition of Boothen Mill in 1881, and a rescued altar are conserved in the churchyard.

Leaving Trentham, the river dodges beneath the A34. The old coach road followed the east bank of the river from Hanford via Stone to cross the river at Wolseley Bridge. Around 1600, after repeated problems with flooding, a narrow pack-horse bridge north of Stone at Darlaston was widened, and the route altered to take advantage of higher ground west of the river. In 1799, a coach bound for Liverpool left the road and overturned in the Trent, drowning three passengers. Today, the modern road barely notices the river, by-passing Stone, to the west, switching banks briefly at Darlaston Park and sweeping back again at Meaford on modern concrete spans.

The bustling little market town of Stone developed as a busy canal port when the Trent and Mersey Canal opened. Although set back from the immediate floodplain, it is on the lower ground of the east bank and has regularly suffered flooding. Stone was a coaching stop on the road from London and the south to Chester, Holyhead, Liverpool and Manchester, three nights out from London and one night's journey from Chester.

Medieval Walton Bridge on Stafford Road, Stone was replaced in 1984, closed to traffic and is now restricted to pedestrians. The abutments of a narrow 14th-century pack-horse bridge can still be traced beneath the pointed arches. A riverside path runs through water meadows north of the bridge. Downstream the

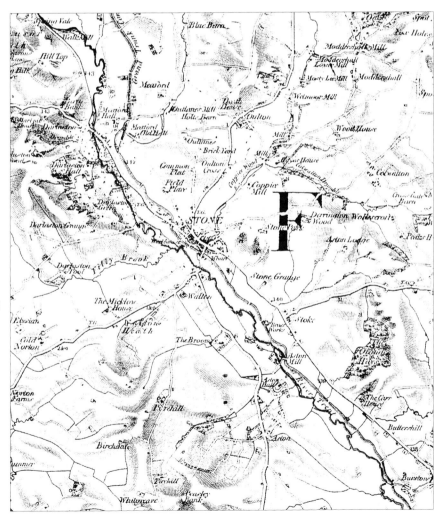

62   *Darlaston and Stone to Burston.*

63 *Markers define the local canoe club's slalom course below Walton Bridge at Stone.*

64 *A steel footbridge links Burston village with a wetland site now managed and protected for the benefit of wildlife. The bridge crosses the Trent at the point where Jolpool Brook empties into the river. An axle from a mill that once stood nearby is displayed in the village centre (inset).*

water swirls and boils beneath markers strung overhead to define a slalom course enjoyed by local canoe club enthusiasts.

Beyond the A51 platform the river encounters a tiny hump-backed brick bridge at Aston-by-Stone. Similar in design to an adjacent canal bridge, it was probably built at the same

time in the 1770s, replacing a medieval bridge. Between Aston and Burston a trail leads through farmland managed and protected by Severn Trent Water plc for the benefit of wildlife. With farming and conservation hand-in-hand, snipe, lapwing and otter are among the rare species to have benefited. A galvanised, tubular steel footbridge across the Trent links a specially created wetland site to Burston.

Burston is a hidden gem nestling in a loop of the river where Jolpool Brook meets the Trent. Two tiny triangular greens at the village centre are surrounded by elegant Georgian houses and an older property, timber-framed with herringbone brick infilling. St Rufin's Chapel stands beside a row of cottages opposite the millpond. Burston Hall was rebuilt in Georgian style after being destroyed by fire in the early 19th century.

Sandon's 15th-century bridge was rebuilt after flood damage in 1947. North of the river, beyond the canal and A51, are the grounds of Sandon Park. A Doric column with an urn, erected in 1806 as a memorial to former prime minister, William Pitt the Younger, is visible through the trees.

A road bridge leads to the village of Salt and Hopton Heath, a low, moorland plateau scarred and pitted by old coal diggings. In one of many Civil War engagements played out in the Trent Valley, Royalist cavalry commanded by Spencer Compton, Earl of Northampton routed a much larger force of Parliamentarians. During the battle the Earl's horse stumbled. Refusing to ask for quarter he was killed. Compton's body was offered in exchange for captured artillery, a violation of convention dismissed as outrageous by the Cavaliers.

A single-arched stone bridge at Weston on the road to Stafford dates from around 1800. It replaced a medieval bridge that stood for at least five hundred years and is on the site of an ancient ford. St Andrew's Church has been much restored but retains a fine early 13th-century tower. Dorothy, daughter of Robert Devereux, 2nd Earl of Essex probably built Weston Hall on the gentle slopes of Weston Bank in the mid-17th century. Derelict in the 1990s, it has now been restored to Elizabethan Gothic splendour and opened as a hotel and restaurant in 2001. In the 19th century, a giant carp weighing 19½ lbs was caught in a Trent-fed lake in the grounds.

Saline springs around Weston in use in medieval times were exploited on an industrial scale from the 17th century. Shirleywich, named after the Shirley lords of Chartley, was once known more prosaically as 'Brine Pits'. Salt was an important preservative in the days before refrigeration. Water from springs was piped into reservoirs. Natural evaporation strengthened the solution before it was run off into boiling pans. The resulting brownish crystals of sodium chloride were whitened using egg white or bullocks' blood. Strings of pack-horses carried salt across the Midlands before the waterways took over after the opening of the Trent and Mersey Canal. Boat owner James Sutton of Shardlow, quick to recognise a profitable opportunity, bought the salt works belonging to William Moore of Wychdon Lodge. Shirleywich Canal Arm, cut in 1810, linked the factory directly to the Trent and Mersey. Salt works, opened at Weston in the 1820s, were soon producing two hundred and fifty tons of salt weekly. Salt merchants in Cheshire, among the backers of

65 *The Trent below Sandon Bridge runs through rich pastureland typical of rural Staffordshire.*

the Trent and Mersey Canal, took advantage of access to the Trent Navigation to transport enormous quantities. A salt warehouse was built as a collection and distribution point at Horninglow Basin, Burton-on-Trent. Declining demand made the smaller scale Trentside salt works of Staffordshire no longer viable. Closure came as the 20th century dawned.

Below Weston, traces of a dismantled railway between Stafford and Uttoxeter are barely discernible. A small bridge carries a farm track across the river and there are road bridges to Ingestre and Tixall before an aqueduct carries the Staffordshire and Worcestershire Canal to its junction with the Trent and Mersey.

A deer park was enclosed at Ingestre in 1417. The grounds were landscaped in typically naturalistic style by leading designer Lancelot 'Capability' Brown in 1756 and now accommodate a golf course. Jacobean Ingestre Hall, used as a residential arts centre by Sandwell Borough Council, stands in mannered contrast to the simple, spare splendour of St Mary's Church, built for Walter Chetwynd in 1676 and attributed to Christopher Wren, although firm evidence to confirm the attribution has proved elusive.

On its journey through the farmland of north Staffordshire the twisting, turning Trent curls over weirs and beneath low-slung pipe

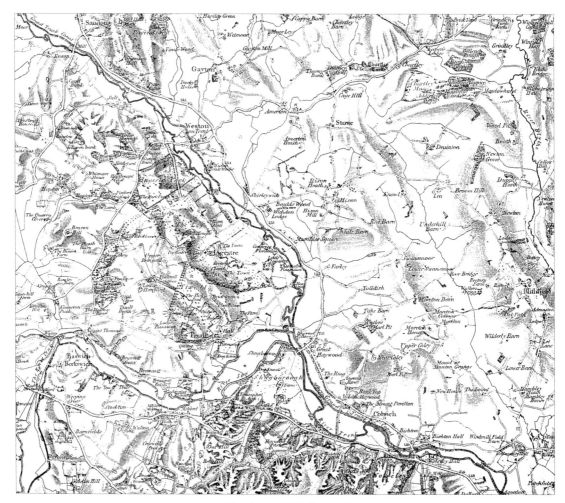

66   *Sandon to Wolseley Bridge.*

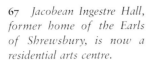

67 *Jacobean Ingestre Hall, former home of the Earls of Shrewsbury, is now a residential arts centre.*

68 *Essex Bridge at Great Haywood replaced a wooden footbridge in the 16th or 17th century. Cutwaters between each of the remaining 14 arches help prevent scouring. The bridge is around one hundred yards in length but barely four feet wide with low parapets.*

bridges closely accompanied by the Trent and Mersey Canal. Almost an adjunct to the scene, it slips by largely unnoticed. All the time the volume of water is steadily growing. Swollen by Gayton Brook, Amerton Brook, Jolpool Brook, Salt Brook and countless smaller streams, the Trent collects the River Sow at Shugborough to become a substantial river. Meece Brook, a tributary of the Sow, runs close to Izaak Walton's timber-framed cottage at Shallowford, now a museum dedicated to angling. Walton, the son of an innkeeper, was born in Stafford in 1593. He moved to London as a child, was apprenticed to a clothier and ran his own ironmongery and linen drapery businesses as well as writing acclaimed biographies of John

Donne among others. After retiring from trade – 'I have laid aside business, and gone afishing' – he returned to the Staffordshire countryside, buying Halfhead Farm Estate including the cottage in 1654, a year after *The Compleat Angler* was published. 'I love any discourse of rivers, and fish and fishing', he wrote. A rare mix of practical advice, philosophical meditation and celebration of rural England made Walton's guide to the delights of fishing an enduring classic.

Sir Walter Raleigh is popularly supposed to have spread his cloak before Queen Elizabeth to protect her feet from a puddle. Robert Devereux, 1st Earl of Essex (1567–1601) may have upstaged him by building Essex Bridge immediately downstream of the confluence with the River Sow in time for a royal visit. One hundred yards long but barely four feet wide, Essex Bridge creates a strange, larger than life sense of scale, reminiscent of Gulliver in Lilliput. Low parapets with pedestrian refuges may have been designed to allow packhorses with panniers slung either side to cross in single file. Cutwaters between each of the 14 remaining arches protect the bridge from scouring and erosion. Although known as Essex Bridge and sometimes as Queen's Bridge (as well as Haywood Bridge locally), the structure strongly suggests 17th-century rather than Tudor origins. It may have supplanted an earlier wooden bridge serving a palace belonging to the Bishops of Lichfield that once stood nearby. Even so it is fun to imagine that its inspiration was a gallant act to impress by an ambitious royal favourite. It may have occurred to the young Devereux that a bridge would be useful for taking his hounds and horses from the Essex estate at Chartley Hall to hunt on Cannock Chase.

69 Shugborough Hall, ancestral home of the Anson family, stands close to the confluence of the Trent and Sow.

70 Modern Wolseley Bridge was built after a much damaged and patched up medieval bridge (inset) collapsed in 1798.

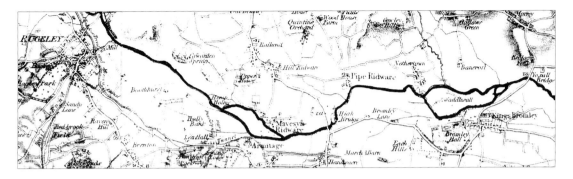

71   *Rugeley to Yoxall.*

72   *High Bridge near Handsacre, an iron span made by the Coalbrookdale Company of Ironbridge in 1830.*

Viscount Anson remodelled his home at Shugborough Hall in the early 19th century and extended the park. An ambitious landscaping programme re-routed the River Sow, diverted a road and moved what remained of Shugborough village. Trent Lane Cottages, lining the approach to Essex Bridge at Great Haywood, were built to house displaced tenants.

South of Shugborough, the river loops south, caressing the thickly wooded fringe of Cannock Chase and passing beneath a railway bridge and narrow, cobbled Weetman's Bridge at Little Haywood, built in 1888 and named after Joseph Weetman, the main subscriber.

Medieval Wolseley Bridge was damaged beyond repair in 1795, its surviving arches were blasted and the debris was cleared. A temporary replacement collapsed with some loss of life just three years later and the present substantial stone bridge of three arches was built.

Approaching Rugeley, a sturdy aqueduct carries the Trent and Mersey Canal across the river at Brindley Bank. Passing under a modern road bridge and two railway bridges, the river skirts Brereton and Armitage. Open fields and rural views to the east contrast with industrial build-up on the western side of the river dominated by Rugeley Power Station and the factory of Armitage Shanks, a name familiar from the company's trademark sanitary ware. Hemp Holm, an area of wetland, is a reminder of pre-Industrial Revolution days before cheap cotton textiles became widely available and most clothes were a hempen mix. In Tudor times, farmers were

instructed to set aside a minimum of one acre to grow hemp nettles, also called 'gallows grass' or 'neck weed', because ropes woven from hemp fibres were used in public hangings.

A Victorian footbridge leads to Mavesyn Ridware across a damp field dimpled with bays left by medieval fishponds. Mavesyn Ridware Hall was home to the Mavesyn (or Malvoison) family until the last of the male line, Sir Robert, was slain in 1403 at the Battle of Shrewsbury fighting beside Henry IV. Unable to wait for the official start of hostilities, Sir Robert killed his neighbour, Sir William Handsacre, a supporter of Henry Hotspur's rebels, in a riverside fight before setting off to join King Henry. The house passed by marriage through female descendants to the Cawardens and later the Chadwicks. Much of the 14th-century gatehouse was retained when the hall was rebuilt in 1718. Monuments and memorials to generations of these families fill the Mavesyn Chapel in St Nicholas's Church. Aerial survey of the riverside east of the hall identified a Neolithic causewayed camp.

In addition to 'Mavesyn', three other small villages in the area, 'Pipe', 'Hill', and 'Hamstall', all have the suffix 'Ridware' meaning 'river people'.

An attractive single-span iron bridge set on masonry bastions near Handsacre was made by the Coalbrookdale Company, makers of the ground-breaking first iron bridge that now forms the centrepiece of Ironbridge Gorge Museum in Shropshire. Built in 1830 when Coalbrookdale were experimenting with artistic forms, High Bridge is light and graceful. Originally two wooden bridges crossed the river here. A stone bridge followed in the 17th century. High Bridge is now sidelined beside a rather less distinguished but functional concrete road bridge.

After passing under a footbridge at Nethertown, the river divides into two arms. The more northerly gathers the River Blithe while a shallower branch passes alongside a former gravel pit, now used by a sailing club, and over two fords close to the village of King's Bromley before reuniting with its fellow on the approach to Yoxall. In between the two fords, a curved weir reveals where a stream drew water to turn the wheel of a now vanished mill.

Yoxall Bridge, reportedly in urgent need of repair in 1662, managed to survive until 1998 when a modern bridge replaced it. The old stone bridge now stands in serene retirement alongside the new crossing.

Five

By Water and the Wood:
The National Forest and Burton upon Trent to Shardlow

Second World War pillboxes line the Trent at regular intervals on its journey through the low-lying washlands of East Staffordshire and South Derbyshire, all built in a 12-month period that began in the summer of 1940 when a full-scale German invasion was a serious possibility. They were designed to guard potential crossing points, using the river as a defensive barrier to slow down an enemy advance and buy vital time.

Between Alrewas and Wychnor, the tiny River Swarbourn joins the Trent before river and Trent and Mersey Canal briefly unite below Alrewas Lock. Five-storey Alrewas Mill, a former cotton-spinning factory, is now converted into riverside apartments. A 250-yard stretch of watery level crossing spanned by a long towpath bridge, ends at a large curving weir protected by a safety boom.

This part of the Trent Valley has a reputation as the 'thunder capital' of England. Historically it has been subject to frequent flooding. Alrewas turned its floodplain to advantage by cultivating extensive osier beds. Basket weaving was an important local cottage industry until modern times. Old pollarded willows and coppiced osier beds can still be seen in surrounding fields. In 1967, houses in Alrewas became the first in the United Kingdom to have their appliances adapted to use natural gas, delivered by pipeline from reserves beneath the North Sea.

The National Forest Company, formed in 1996, has created vast swathes of new woodland through east Staffordshire, south Derbyshire and

north-west Leicestershire. Within a decade, over five million saplings have been planted as part of a long-term project to restore a landscape scarred by mining and heavy industry.

The manor of Wychnor was granted to Robert de Somerville after the Norman Conquest. In a triangle of land between river and canal the outline of a moat shows where the manor house of the Somervilles and their Griffith heirs stood until Tudor times. Depressions

74 *A line of riverside pillboxes through East Staffordshire and South Derbyshire was built in 1940/1 when an invasion by German forces was considered a serious threat.*

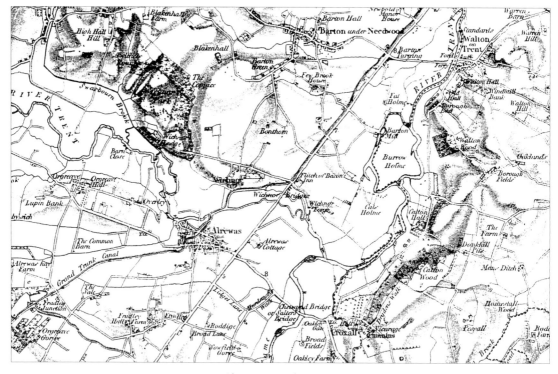

75   *Alrewas to Walton-on-Trent.*

left by fishponds and the ditches that once fed water to power a corn mill can still be seen alongside. In 1584, the foundations for a new house were laid out well away from the flood-plain, on an escarpment looking out over the river to the spires of Lichfield Cathedral. Much rebuilt over the years, the house and grounds are now home to Wychnor Park Country Club. Further along the ridge, the ghosts of house platforms either side of a central track mark the site of a deserted medieval village. Nearby is the church of St Leonard, parts of which date back to *c.*1200.

The A38 trunk road follows the line of Roman Ryknield Street crossing the river at Wychnor on a flat concrete deck. Roman road builders laid a causeway on a foundation of oak pilings across the marshy ground leading to a ford or bridge. A series of narrow stone arches known collectively as Wychnor Bridges had been built by the 13th century. The main section is referred to as 'King's Bridge' in early

quarter session reports. Before a wider bridge was built in 1795, passengers by coach faced the inconvenience of walking across while their carriages used a deep ford.

Swinfen Canoe Club meets on a section of river south of the A38. Sweeping beneath two railway viaducts in quick succession the Trent accepts the River Tame. Mythaholme steel footbridge links riverside paths to the 16-acre site of the National Memorial Arboretum where fifty thousand trees form a living tribute to those touched by two world wars and more recent conflicts.

This is the Trent at its most southerly. From here the river journey is north and east. Old watercourses create the low-lying islands of Cat Holme, Cherry Holme, and Borough Holme. Extensive mineral extraction has left numerous small lakes in the valley that now provide wildlife friendly habitats. Croxall Lakes Nature Reserve, where the River Mease stumbles into the Trent, is one example. Landscaped pastoral lushness surrounds Catton Hall. The house, beside a beautiful curve of the river, has been in the same family for six centuries. Venerable oak trees in the grounds remember most of the generations.

An ancient ford at Walton-on-Trent played a crucial role in 1322, when a power struggle between Thomas, Earl of Lancaster, then the most powerful noble in England, and Edward II developed into open rebellion. Lancaster occupied Burton-on-Trent and barricaded the bridge waiting for reinforcements to arrive. With the river running high after heavy rain it was a strong defensive position. A frustrating situation for the King was resolved by a little local knowledge. He was shown the ford upstream at Walton-on-Trent where a safe crossing was possible. While a detachment of archers led a diversionary attack on the bridge at Burton, the main army crossed the river. Outflanked and surprised by the manoeuvre, Lancaster fled. Edward gave thanks for his success in the bridge

chapel before setting out in pursuit. Defeat at Burton-on-Trent effectively ended Lancaster's revolt. Within weeks the Earl had been captured and executed.

A ferry at Walton-on-Trent operated until 1835 when an issue of £10 shares raised sufficient money to pay for a bridge. Tolls were charged until 1900. The board detailing the scale of charges is now stored in the bell-ringing room at St Lawrence's Church. Since the floods of 1947 swept away the bridge, a series of Bailey Bridges anchored on the 19th-century masonry piers limits the crossing to cars and light vans. Despite notices warning of width and weight restrictions, drivers of large vehicles unfamiliar with the area are regularly trapped on the narrow approach road.

Drakelow is named after *Dracan Hlaw* or 'Dragon's Low', indicating a burial mound. A small sixth-century earthenware bowl of a type usually associated with burials was discovered here. Drakelow Hall was home to the Gresley

76 *Drakelow Hall with its attractive riverside terrace was demolished in the 1950s and Drakelow Power Station built in the grounds.*

family from the Norman Conquest until it was sold in 1933. Although much altered in the 18th and 19th centuries, the hall retained an essentially Elizabethan appearance until it was demolished in the early 1950s to make way for Drakelow Power Station. Clipped yew hedges, rose gardens, elaborate fountains, tennis courts and manicured lawns scrolling down to the water's edge were bulldozed into oblivion.

Winding between Drakelow and Branston, where a lost ford once carried the Roman *Via Devana* from Leicester to Chester, the river passes beneath the 'Leicester Line' railway bridge to reach Burton-on-Trent, a town that gained a

reputation in the 19th century as the brewing capital of the world. Beside the Fleet, a silted weed-choked arm of the Trent, little remains of the Benedictine monastery that dominated life in the town for more than five hundred years. Part of the infirmary chapel is home to Burton Club and attached to the *Abbey Inn*, a largely Victorian refurbishment but with some old timbers and earlier features. Burton College occupies the site of Soho Wharf. A few stone blocks, some with rusted mooring rings attached, are all that can be seen today of a once flourishing port at the head of the Trent Navigation.

77 *In the 18th century, the Navigation was extended inland and a wharf was built on the site of Burton's former Benedictine abbey beside an arm of the river known as the Fleet. A private house incorporating the former monastic infirmary occupied the site in Victorian times.* Burton Club and the Abbey Inn *now share the building.*

78 *A few stone blocks with mooring rings attached are visible at the former Soho Wharf site at Burton-on-Trent.*

79   *The Ferry Bridge at Burton-on-Trent was completed in 1889. It replaced a ferry (inset) struggling to deal with passenger demand. A year after the bridge opened a cast-iron viaduct was added, leading over flood-prone washlands to the town centre.*

A ferry at Stapenhill operated from the Middle Ages. By 1864, two flat-bottomed punts were carrying over five thousand passengers between Stapenhill and Burton-on-Trent each week. The ferry operated under licence from the Marquess of Anglesey, a descendant of William, 6th Baron Paget who acquired shipping rights on the Trent at Burton by Act of Parliament in 1698. In 1865, the Marquess obtained a further Act authorising a bridge but took no action. Numbers using the ferry reached 12,000 a week by the mid-1880s. Local brewery magnate, Michael Arthur Bass (1st Baron Burton from 1886), offered to finance construction of a footbridge if Burton-on-Trent Borough Council purchased the rights from the Marquess. A 240-ft wrought-iron latticework bridge of three spans carried on the suspension principle opened in 1889. Dignitaries attending the official opening crossed on the last ferry. Within a year a new cast-iron viaduct replaced a plank walkway that led over the flood-prone washlands from the new Ferry Bridge. The cost of acquiring the rights was to be recouped by

a toll and the bridge was closed overnight from 11 p.m. In 1898 Lord Burton again came to the aid of the town and paid off the outstanding balance. St Peter's Bridge, a much-needed second road bridge, opened alongside in 1985.

A tree-lined riverside walk and municipal gardens occupy higher ground on the Stapenhill bank where St Peter's Church stands on a low riverside bluff. Swans gather in large numbers, attracted by the promise of titbits from people enjoying a stroll by the riverside.

Recent flood prevention and drainage schemes provided an opportunity to develop washlands west of the river as a wildlife habitat and recreational area. Side channels produce a number of islands. Colourful marquees crowd the riverside meadows each July for a two-day regatta held jointly by Burton Leander Rowing Club (founded 1847) and Trent Rowing Club (established in the 1860s).

Generations of Burtonians learned to swim in the river at Alligator Point, now no longer a discernible feature. Bathing sheds on the Hay meadow were replaced by public swimming baths beside Burton Bridge in 1875. The Victorian baths remained in use until the Meadowside Leisure Centre opened in 1980 and the old pools were demolished.

Andresey (Andrew's Isle), the site of a chapel founded, according to tradition, by St Modwen in the seventh century, was linked to the town centre in 1884 by a decorative iron footbridge. Tucked discreetly into a stone well beside the bridge is a weathered carving of the Paget family crest – heraldic tigers supporting a shield of eagles and lions – a commemoration of the local lords of the manor rescued when the old town hall was demolished.

The strategic importance of Burton-on-Trent's Great Bridge made it the focus of conflict during the Civil War and the town changed hands a number of times. In 1643, Colonel Thomas Tyldesley wrested Burton temporarily from Parliamentarian control by leading a daring cavalry assault across the narrow bridge. Queen Henrietta Maria witnessed the gallant colonel's charge and rewarded him with a knighthood.

Stone footings for the Great Bridge of Burton-on-Trent were probably laid soon after the founding of the abbey c.1002. A more convenient crossing of the River Trent than the fords that allowed access at various points was essential to the establishment of an influential religious centre and a viable settlement. Eventually, 36 arches carried a 16-ft wide causeway for five hundred yards across three separate arms of the river and the small island of Broadholme. Approaching Winshill a gently curving line was introduced following a natural bend along the Derbyshire bank over the Trundle Hole, a lagoon-like inlet that silted up and disappeared completely in the 19th century. Stone for the bridge was brought from a quarry downstream between Winshill and Newton Solney.

In 1859, George Hudson, go-ahead chairman of the Midland Railway Company, obtained an Act of Parliament authorising a replacement for the narrow medieval bridge. In return for being relieved of all future maintenance liabilities, the Marquess of Anglesey paid a third of the construction costs. Burton-on-Trent's new crossing was opened with a fanfare of publicity in 1864. A few years later the old bridge was demolished.

Burton Meadow, a recreational area, can be reached by a side road from the bridge or across a new footbridge, built as part of a walkway created for the millennium. Horse races on Burton Meadow were abandoned in 1841 after a vigorous campaign led by a local vicar highlighted disorderly behaviour amongst spectators. Stone from the grandstand was recycled to build a new frontage for the Congregational Chapel in the town's High Street.

80 *Two separate branches of the river meet around Andresey Island, Burton-on-Trent. The right-hand channel and an inlet known as 'Alligator Point' (no longer a discernible feature) were once popular public swimming areas.*

81   *A replacement for Burton-on-Trent's historic 'Great Bridge' opened in 1864. Shortly afterwards the medieval bridge was demolished.*

82   *In 1780, at the start of the Industrial Revolution, Robert Peel (grandfather of Robert Peel, Prime Minister 1834-5 and 1841-6) moved his mechanised cotton spinning operation from Lancashire to Staffordshire. Peel Mill, the first of five textile mills built along the river at Burton-on-Trent, stands on an artificial island.*

At Winshill, the river barrels over a weir at a former mill site. Water-powered turbines ground flour here until 1991. Wrapped inside the current renovation is the ghost of a Saxon mill owned by the monks of Burton Abbey. A four-storey cotton mill, built on an artificial island next to the flour mill for Robert Peel in 1780, shared the weir and sluices. Peel moved to Burton after angry hand spinners smashed the spinning jennies installed in his Blackburn factory. Mass produced cotton, colourful as silk but a fraction of the price, soon overtook worsted cloth as the material of choice for everyday wear. By 1800 the textile industry was the main employer in the area. The Peel family opened a further four

mills along the Trent locally. Robert Peel junior, father of the Prime Minister, expanded along the River Tame to Tamworth.

Modern landscape maps of the Trent Valley show many dry or seasonal channels marked 'Old Trent Water' and river-hugging boundaries that nose unexpectedly into fields – clues to changes in the flow, some due to manmade changes to control flooding or improve navigation, others the result of natural processes. The most ambitious, if fictional, design to alter the route of the river occurs in Act 3 of Shakespeare's *Henry IV Part One*. In a vivid scene, Henry Hotspur, Edmund Mortimer, and Owen Glendower are plotting rebellion. It is

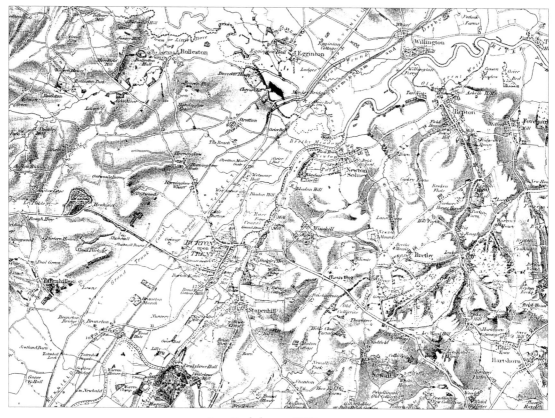

83   *Drakelow to Willington.*

1403 and a map of the kingdom is spread out before them. They are discussing how they will divide the kingdom: land to the west of the River Severn for Glendower, south of the Trent for Mortimer, north of the Trent for Hotspur. Shakespeare's source material was Raphael Holinshed's *Chronicles of England, Scotland and Ireland*, first published in 1577. Shakespeare has Hotspur complain about his proposed share in the following terms:

> Methinks, my moiety, north from Burton here,
> In quantity equals not one of yours;
> See, how this river comes me cranking in,
> And cuts me, from the best of my land,
> A huge half moon, a monstrous cantle out.
> I'll have the current in this place dammed up;
> And here the smug and silver Trent shall run,
> In a new channel fair and evenly:
> It shall not wind with such a deep indent,
> To rob me of so rich a bottom here.

Inspired by Shakespeare's words, Sir John Alfred Arnesby Brown painted *The Smug and Silver Trent* (Birmingham Museums and Art Gallery) in 1924, using Burton Stather as the location. In the context of the scene, Shakespeare has to mean Burton-on-Trent. Here the river reaches its southernmost point before capriciously flowing northwards. Hotspur's threat to dam the channel and change its course due east to the Wash would have netted him half of Nottinghamshire and most of Lincolnshire (it would also have returned the river to its pre-Ice-Age route through the Vale of Belvoir). Any change at Burton Stather, just three miles from Trent Falls and the Humber would make little difference.

After a Civil War skirmish north of the river at Egginton, several Royalist soldiers were reported drowned as they attempted to flee across an ancient ford at Newton Solney where the River Dove boosts the Trent. Parliamentarian forces regularly patrolled this stretch of the Trent to disrupt communications between Royalist held castles at Tutbury and Ashby-de-la-Zouch.

Looping and winding through the broad valley, crossed by a footbridge and a water pipe drawing supplies from the River Dove to feed Staunton Harold Reservoir eight miles south, the river reaches Willington. A choice of a paved ford or a passenger ferry saved travellers between Willington and neighbouring Repton a long detour via Twyford, where a chain ferry with the capacity to carry livestock and farm waggons

continued to serve the local rural community into the middle of the 20th century. A boat service at Willington is first mentioned in Repton churchwarden accounts for 1600. An Act of Parliament authorising a bridge was passed in 1835. A clause ordered the destruction of the existing ford and ferry – subject to compensation – and fines for any do-it-yourself enthusiasts in order to maximise toll receipts for investors. Private donations and a share issue raised the necessary capital and a graceful five-arched bridge was completed in 1839. Although commercial river traffic had all but ceased above Shardlow, the central arch was designed to allow Upper Trent craft to pass. Tolls applied until 1898 when

84   *Twyford chain ferry served a largely rural local community and was capable of carrying farm waggons or a few head of livestock. It continued to operate until the mid-20th century.*

85   *Sir Francis Burdett and other local dignitaries led a procession across the bridge between Willington and Repton to celebrate the ending of charges in 1898. The tollgates were ceremonially removed. Part of the spiked top rail of the turnpike bar (inset) now guards an entry beside the village post office in Repton.*

Derby County Council agreed to buy Willington Bridge from the trustees. The toll notice was taken down and hung in Repton Church. A section of spiked rail from the tollgate now guards an entrance beside Repton Post Office. The tollhouse was struck by a vehicle in 1958 and subsequently demolished.

Mysterious and romantic, the caves of Anchor Church are hewn in a sandstone and bunter crag. A natural fissure has been extended, creating two separate chambers. The larger has a figure-of-eight ground plan with supporting pillars. Recessed niches are cut into the walls. Doorways at either end provide access and three large windows gaze out across the floodplain. Nearby is a smaller cave known as the Anchorite's Larder. An anchorite was a hermit or religious recluse. Occupation may date from early-Christian Mercia but the first documentary record of an inhabitant is in 1658, when an entry in Repton church register refers to 'Ye foole at Anchor Church'. In the 18th century, local squire Sir Robert Burdett of Foremark Hall added doors and fitted out the caves as an unusual dining room for the entertainment of dinner guests.

A 15th-century riverside farmhouse at Ingleby was converted into the *John Thompson* public house in 1969 and now has its own small brewery. The eponymous owner earned an award for bravery from the Humane Society for gallantly attempting to save the life of a man whose car left the road and was swept into the river by floodwater in 1957.

Circling around sand and gravel works the river brushes the edge of Barrow upon Trent and approaches Swarkestone. A medieval causeway across the floodplain is a scheduled ancient monument but it still carries a steady flow of traffic. For centuries the crossing was the major route south from Derby. In the 18th and 19th centuries it was used by London-bound mail coaches. There was a stone bridge across the river here by 1204 and probably a timber platform earlier. Monks from Repton Priory attended a tiny bridge chapel since lost to decay and in subsequent rebuilding and repair work during the 17th century. The present five-arched bridge dates from 1801 when widening was necessary to cope with increased traffic. The long, low causeway retains its medieval character. Seen from below, the first arches at Stanton-by-Bridge

86   *Swarkestone Bridge dates from 1801. The causeway is much older and retains much of its medieval character. Seen from below, the first arches leading from Stanton by Bridge (inset) are supported by chamfered ribs, an innovation first used in 12th-century church architecture.*

are much as they would have been built, each supported by eight chamfered ribs. According to legend, two sisters built the bridge and causeway after their lovers drowned attempting to keep a tryst when the river was in flood.

Swarkestone Hall, home of the Harpur family, stood east of the crossing beyond St James's Church. At the start of the Civil War, Sir John Harpur became a colonel in the Royalist army under the command of Sir Henry Hastings. The hall was garrisoned to guard Swarkestone Bridge but a determined assault by Parliamentarian troops routed defending forces and Swarkestone Hall was destroyed in an act of reprisal. An eye-catching three-storey pavilion, used for recreational sports such as bowls and possibly as a spectator grandstand for deer coursing, was left intact. In more recent times the building appeared on a Rolling Stones' album cover.

Swarkestone Bridge was the most southerly point reached by the Highland forces of Bonnie Prince Charlie during the Jacobite rebellion of 1745. Expected support had failed to materialise and a lukewarm response to the Stuart cause from the landed gentry of the Trent Valley may have disheartened the Pretender. Some have blamed the flat, featureless terrain for fading morale. In 1995, U.A. Fanthorpe began a poem about the decision to turn back with the words: 'He turned back here. Anyone would.' Whatever the reason, the river played a role in this pivotal moment in British history. When Charles Edward Stuart reached the Trent, the Hanoverian royal family already had their bags packed. Fanthorpe concludes: 'London stood open as jelly. Nobody could have stopped him. This place did.'

Fanthorpe's poem talks of turnip fields but this sheltered part of the Trent Vale with its gentle rolling hills and rich, loamy soil supported a variety of crops and was an important market gardening area.

Weston-on-Trent developed on the Derbyshire bank of the river close to an important ford and ferry crossing at King's Mills. Like many of the Trent's rural ferry services, the boat operated until the Second World War. For

87   *When Parliamentarian forces destroyed the Trentside home of Royalist Sir John Harpur after defeating his forces in a skirmish at Swarkestone Bridge, this three-storey, twin-towered Jacobean 'pavilion' was left intact.*

a couple of years from 1923, a second ferry was introduced at Weston Cliff, where a small wharf was used to ship gypsum from quarries at Chellaston to be ground into plaster at King's Mills. There was a mill here when Domesday Book was compiled. By 1718 mill buildings occupied both banks. In addition to plaster manufacture, papermaking and fulling have taken place over the years as well as grinding corn. A hotel occupies the site today.

Weston-on-Trent became a popular inland resort and recreational destination in the early 20th century. Visitors came in large numbers each weekend by bicycle, charabanc, railway and tram to camp or picnic by the river. Special trains ran from Derby at midday each Saturday when factory buzzers announced the end of the working week. There was a bathing lido upstream of a weir at King's Mills. Rowing boats could be hired. Pleasure boats cruised between King's Mills and an oxbow lake known as Black Pool by Weston Cliff. Fishing was popular. Until 1914, the occasional salmon was

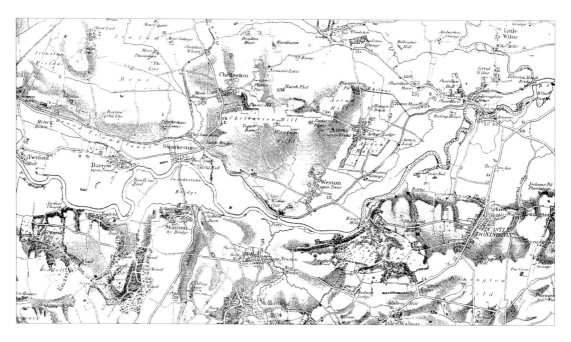

88 *A hotel now occupies the site of the former mill complex at King's Mills. Flour, plaster, paper, and felt have all been produced here in the past. A ford was closed in the early 20th century putting additional pressure on a chain ferry operated by Polly Rowbottom (inset) that continued to run until the middle of the 20th century.*

89 *Twyford to Derwent Mouth.*

landed. Eels were plentiful and the catch from a series of 10 traps attached to the weir was packed in barrels and sent to London.

Closure of the ford at King's Mills in the early 20th century put additional pressure on the ferry. Travellers between Weston-on-Trent and Castle Donington, King's Newton, and Melbourne faced delays and inconvenience. Trent College Officer Training Corps, based

in Derby, provided a temporary solution by building two narrow suspension bridges that served for a number years. During the Second World War, members of the Royal Engineers and units from other Allied Forces divisions based at Weston-on-Trent erected and dismantled prefabricated Bailey Bridges destined for use in Europe after the D-Day landings, on an almost daily basis. A redundant railway viaduct leading across flood-prone Burnett's Fields to a box-girder bridge is now part of the Cloud Trail footpath and cycleway.

Behind wooded hills lies Castle Donington. Donington Park racing circuit and East Midlands Airport are close by. The Earl of Chester put the 'Castle' in Castle Donington, building a motte and bailey stronghold to command the river crossing at King's Mills, soon after the Norman Conquest. In the 15th century, William, Lord Hastings leased the castle and its lands from the Crown. His descendant, Sir George Hastings, bought the estate outright in 1595. Abandoning the castle he plundered its stonework to build Donington Hall, set in 400 acres of beautiful parkland stretching down to riverside cliffs and stocked with fallow deer.

In 1908 the last vestige of castle wall disappeared, leaving just the mound at the north edge of the village. Francis Rawdon Hastings, 2nd Earl of Moira, built the present Donington Hall in 1790. In the First World War the mansion became a prisoner-of-war camp for German officers and was requisitioned again by the Government in 1939. Between the wars it was used as a hotel attached to the racing circuit. British Midland Airways now have their headquarters at the hall. The wild deer herd and some veteran oak trees, old enough to remember the arrival of the Hastings family, survive in an area of the park now designated a Site of Special Scientific Interest and managed subject to Countryside Stewardship Scheme regulations.

Sir Henry Hastings (created Lord Loughborough in 1643) was a leading supporter of the King in the Civil War. Under his direction, defensive earthworks were thrown up around King's Mills and a fort was built near Shardlow to protect river crossings and ensure safe passage for Royalist forces and essential supplies. In a daring raid on the night of 5 February 1644, 30 handpicked men gained entry under cover of darkness and took the King's Mills garrison by surprise. Parliamentarian forces wrested control at Shardlow in July 1644, after a determined attack during which burning haycarts were planted against the fort walls.

For the last decades of the 17th century, the Fosbrooke family of Shardlow leased the ferry at Wilden from Thomas Coke of Melbourne Hall. Having lost the contract to a consortium of Derby businessmen in 1743, Leonard Fosbrooke junior regained control in 1758, when plans for a bridge were at an advanced stage. A bridge not only threatened continuation of the ferry but it was also a potential obstruction to shipping. Despite opposition and setbacks that included footings 'accidentally' rammed by boats, Cavendish tollbridge was completed in 1760. It remained in use until floodwater wrecked a pier in 1947 and the structure collapsed. A single-file Bailey Bridge took its place

90   *Cavendish Bridge at Shardlow, built in 1760 and demolished in 1947 after much of the structure was swept away during severe floods. A slate pediment (inset) rescued from the former tollhouse, listing the charges for using the crossing, is now on roadside display.*

91   *After floods destroyed
Cavendish Bridge in 1947,
a Bailey Bridge temporarily
took its place until a new
crossing was completed in
1956.*

until a new crossing was completed in 1956. The
tollhouse was demolished at the same time as
debris was cleared from the riverbed. A slate
tablet listing charges was rescued and erected
beside the road nearby.

Shardlow's river port upstream of the crossing at Wilden was rapidly eclipsed when the
Trent and Mersey Canal link at Derwent Mouth
opened in 1777. Ropeworks, breweries, maltings and warehouses soon lined new canalside
wharves. The sheer volume of port business
attracted other traders and merchants. In fifty
years the population doubled and doubled again.
Apart from the proliferation of public houses,
facilities struggled to keep pace with growth.
Before St James's Church opened in 1838, villagers travelled upriver by boat each Sunday to take
part in parish services at Aston-on-Trent. The
Honourable John Byng, journeying through the
East Midlands in 1789, remarked in his diary: 'At
Shardlow, are built so many merchants' houses,
wharfs etc., sprinkled with gardens looking upon
the Trent, and to Castle Donington Hill, as
to form as happy a scenery of business and
pleasures as can be survey'd.' Of the *Rose and
Crown* where his party lodged he comments
on the downside: 'The hostler being drunk and
the women of the house sulky' before adding a
more positive afterthought, 'But we had a good
room and our horses sweet hay.'

Shardlow became a conservation area in
1978. With its marina, old warehouses with
distinctive semicircular windows and a number
of elegant Georgian properties built by wealthy
merchants, it retains much of the character of
an inland port. The Salt Warehouse, oldest of
the surviving stores, houses Shardlow Heritage
Centre. Next door, the Clock Warehouse is now
a public house and restaurant, sitting attractively
astride an arm of the canal that enabled barges
to be loaded and unloaded within the building.

Leading canal carrier James Sutton and his
family lived at Broughton House before moving
into Shardlow Hall (now used by Cranfield
University). The Soresby family, of boat owners
Soresby and Flack, lived at what is now the *Lady
in Grey* hotel. A ropery, run by generations of
the Henshall family until closure in 1940, is now
a private house. A narrow avenue of trees still
marks the line of the open-air ropewalk.

James Brindley built Long Horse Bridge
to carry the canal towpath across the Trent
at Derwent Mouth. A concrete walkway that
replaced the wooden trestle bridge in 1932 was
dismantled in 2003 after it became unstable and
dangerous. Close by, a steel girder aqueduct has
conveyed Long Eaton's water supply since 1909
and the M1 motorway roars across the river on
a reinforced concrete deck.

Six

Rolling Along: Nottingham

At Sawley, a bridge and causeway that took the place of a ferry around 1500 was replaced in stone and iron by Harrington Bridge four centuries later. Sawley Cut takes boats through what is now the busiest lock in the country, avoiding the bridge and rejoining the river close to where a railway viaduct and footbridge cross.

Sawley was overtaken in size and importance during the 19th century when its neighbour Long Eaton (originally Anglo-Saxon *Aitone* or 'Town by the water'), developed as a centre of the lace industry. Erewash Canal runs through Long Eaton to connect with the river at Trent Lock. Two public houses straddle the junction. Beyond the lock, Trent Valley Sailing Club makes use of a broad stretch of river. Twin railway viaducts cross on a series of arches, the

lines disappearing into Redhill Tunnels through castellated brickwork entrances reminiscent of Moorish gateways.

Cranfleet Cut bypasses shoals at the mouth of the Soar to lock back into the river opposite Thrumpton Park. Giant cedars, ancient larches and the rise of Wood Hill mask all but the tips of the giant cooling towers of Ratcliffe-on-Soar Power Station.

To celebrate its centenary in 1989, Nottinghamshire County Council opened the 84-mile Trent Valley Way, a footpath following the river's journey through the county. Starting from Trent Meadows, Long Eaton, or alternatively at Thrumpton, the long-distance path continues to West Stockwith where it links up with the Cuckoo Way along the Chesterfield Canal.

92 *Trent Lock is a waterway interchange where the River Soar, Erewash Canal, and Cranfleet Cut meet the Trent in the shadow of Ratcliffe Power Station and Red Hill. Lock Lane from Sawley follows the line of a Roman road, evidence that this has long been an important riverside site.*

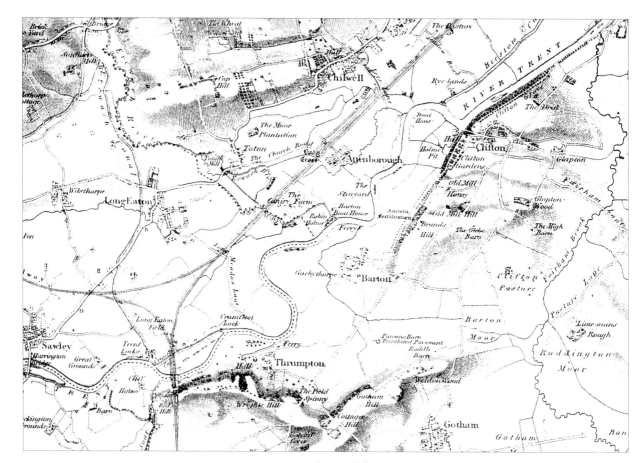

93   *Sawley to Clifton.*

Gervase Pigott of Weston-on-Trent acquired Thrumpton Hall after the Powdrell lords of the manor were convicted of involvement in the Gunpowder Plot of 1605. Discovery of a priest hole, reached by a staircase concealed behind a false chimney, confirmed the Powdrells' Roman Catholic sympathies. Gervase Pigott junior became High Sheriff of Nottinghamshire. He enclosed the park, damming a small tributary of the Trent to create an artificial lake, and enlarged the house, using trees from the estate to produce splendid interior woodwork. In the process he incurred debts that forced his heir to sell the property in 1696 to John Emerton, a London lawyer, whose initials can still be seen on old village cottages. Thrumpton passed to Lucy Emerton Wescomb who married George

Anson, 8th Lord Byron in 1843. Lucy enjoyed Sunday hymns at All Saints Church and is said to have selected servants for the hall on the basis of their singing ability. Death duties forced the sale of half the estate in 1951.

Winding through the flat vale, with Long Eaton and the outskirts of Nottingham in view behind an accompanying railway line, the Trent captures the River Erewash. Henry Ireton, Parliamentary commander in the Civil War and one of the commissioners who signed the death warrant of Charles I, was born in a farmhouse next to the church of St Mary Magdalene at Attenborough. There is a tradition that King Charles crossed by the ferry here on his way to surrender to a Scots army at Southwell in May 1646.

Four decades of sand and gravel extraction at Attenborough began in the 1920s, stripping away osier beds and water meadows. Sensitive management has created a popular attraction where sailing, fishing and other recreational activities sit happily alongside conservation on the 600-acre site. Attenborough Nature Reserve was established in 1966 and designated a Site of Special Scientific Interest in 1982. More than two hundred and fifty different species of birds have been recorded. In the winter, Attenborough is home to large flocks of diving, dabbling wildfowl including pochard, goosander and shoveler.

Barton in Fabis is one of a number of pleasant Trentside villages that, prior to the Second World War, attracted large numbers of visitors keen to spend a summer's day by the river. A ferry continued to make occasional crossings from Attenborough into the 1960s. Floodbanks constructed in 1968 provide protection from the episodic inundations to which the village was once subject. Until the 1940s, when Barton Quay closed and road transport took over, gypsum from Gotham Hills was carried by rail to a jetty for shipment to plaster works along the Trent.

94 *A rowing boat ferried passengers across the river between Thrumpton and Pasture Lane (formerly Long Meadow Lane) leading to Long Eaton. The monogram of John Emerton (inset) who bought Thrumpton Hall in 1696 can be seen on old cottages in the village.*

95 *In Victorian times and in the early part of the 20th century, Barton in Fabis was popular with visitors keen to spend a day by the river. Teas and ice creams were available in the village on summer weekends when the ferry from Attenborough was kept particularly busy.*

Below Barton Island, there are moorings and a marina. Beeston Sailing Club has its headquarters among a number of chalets dotted along the riverbank. Brandshill escarpment fringes the floodplain to the east, a dramatic tree-cloaked rise blending into Rough Wood and Clifton Wood. Brands Hill itself, once known as British Hill, rises to 285 feet. Hardly anything now remains of a series of formidable earth banks that once guarded an Iron-Age enclosure on the summit.

A lock takes river traffic via Beeston, Lenton and the Nottingham Canal to join the river below Trent Bridge. Houses, factories and retail parks spread and thicken towards the centre of Nottingham, an urban prospect leavened by the green swell of Arbour Hill and Wollaton Park. Tumbling over a dogleg weir fitted with a hydro-electric generator the river turns to meet the steep, thickly wooded bank of Clifton Grove, now a local nature reserve stretching behind the Clifton Campus of Nottingham Trent University. 'Clifton Grove, sweet Clifton Grove, a beautiful walk is Clifton Grove' runs the refrain to a once popular song, composed by Jimmy Tongue, a travelling musician.

Alternate layers of grey and red sedimentary rock are exposed near the top of the escarpment. Sandwiched between the Trent and the A453, Old Clifton Village has remained delightfully isolated from the expansion that has taken place all around since Clifton became part of the City of Nottingham in 1951. In a scene barely changed since the days of Queen Anne, a charming row of almshouses overlook the ample green with its large brick dovecote centrepiece. Behind the later brick elevations of thatched cottages lie timber-framed late medieval hall houses.

Clifton Grove was first planted with trees around 1740. The broad ride, part of the River Trent Greenway, is trimmed with oak, ash, sycamore, lime and beech, through which there are glimpses of the river sparkling below. A local folk tale tells of Margaret, the unfaithful 'Fair Maid of Clifton', either thrown into the depths by her seducer or else driven to suicide by shame according to your choice of versions.

96 *The number of chalets along the riverside upstream of Beeston Weir has grown and a marina has been added since this picture was taken around 1910. In the misty background is the wooded bank of Clifton Grove.*

97 *The trees of Clifton Grove were originally planted around 1740. Always a popular leisure walk, a broad ride along the top of the escarpment is now part of the River Trent Greenway and a nature reserve.*

98 *Wilford to Holme Pierrepont.*

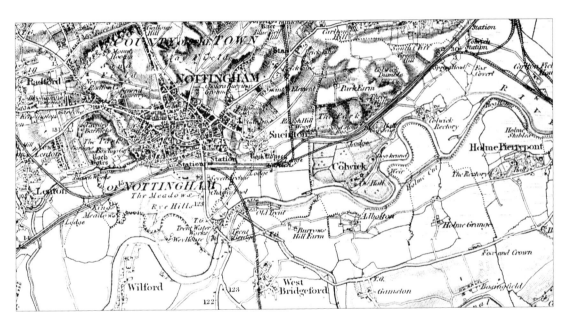

Beyond sports fields on the floodplain of the northern bank are an industrial complex and the buildings of Nottingham University. Fairham Brook empties into the Trent just before the river narrows to pass under the multi-level interchange of Clifton Bridge. A few aspen trees tremble in the breeze, their sibilant murmur drowned by the constant hiss and hum of traffic.

A single cantilever concrete span built soon after Clifton became part of the City of Nottingham in 1952 has since been extended.

Concrete piers are sprayed with multi-coloured graffiti. The riverside here is unkempt but it contains a wide variety of plants. Among disorderly brambles, nettles, thistles, hogweed, water dock, red clover and mugwort, there are also teasel, medick, mallow, tansy, winter-cress, cranesbill and yarrow.

At Wilford, the city begins to close about the river. Houses and waterfront apartments shelter behind floodbanks. Beside St Wilfrid's Church, squat and grey, steps lead down to the

99   *Wilford Bridge, financed by Sir Robert Juckes Clifton and bearing the Clifton family arms, opened in 1870 and was soon dubbed 'Ha'penny Bridge' by locals. A board on the former tollhouse displays a list of the old charges. Nottingham City Council took over the bridge in 1969. It closed to vehicles in 1974.*

water's edge. Opposite on Queen's Drive are the equally squat and grey stubby pylons of North Wilford electricity generating site. Downstream, the Trent swallows the culverted River Leen. Until the 1960s, the Leen emptied into the Nottingham Canal. Discharge was diverted to Wilford to counter the threat of storm water being trapped behind the defences after flood barriers along the Trent were raised.

The Ferry Inn, Wilford, incorporates parts of a 14th-century farmhouse. Originally the *Punch Bowl*, it was renamed in 1864, not long before Wilford chain ferry ceased operations. Crowds once flocked to an annual cherry festival hosted by the inn during the first week of July. White painted stakes lined the path leading across the Meadows to the ferry landing stage, to help passengers find their way in poor light or when the fields were flooded.

A temporary wooden footbridge replaced the ferry while the iron girders of a tollbridge were set in place. Paid for by Sir Robert Juckes Clifton and opened by Lady Clifton in 1870, a year after the death of Sir Robert, locals soon dubbed it 'Ha'penny Bridge'. A board above the entrance to the former tollhouse displays a list of the former charges. The Clifton family motto, *Tenez le droit* ('Hold the right') and coat of arms are emblazoned on the ironwork,

supplied by Andrew Handyside and Company of Derby. Sir Robert's statue stands on a plinth beside the river.

Wilford Bridge relieved some of the pressure on Trent Bridge and was a direct route for traffic into Clifton Colliery where production began the year the bridge was built. Nottingham City Council took ownership of Wilford Bridge in 1969. Five years later it was closed to vehicles. After the replacement of a weakened central span it re-opened as a footbridge.

Looping around the Meadows, once the grim slum underbelly of the growing city and the subject of considerable investment and rebuilding in recent years, the riverside has a neatly manicured expanse of grass threaded with lime trees and steps that double as walkway and flood defence. The parkland of Victoria Embankment was landscaped and donated to the city by Jesse Boot, of Boot's the Chemists fame, in 1920. Born in Nottingham in 1850, Boot was running his own small herbalist shop at the age of 14 and formed J. Boot and Company by 1883. In 1888, the business became Boots Pure Drug Company and began manufacturing their own brand products in addition to retailing. A summerhouse belonging to Sir Jesse Boot (Lord Trent from 1929) opposite the embankment was demolished in 1961.

100 *An impressive monumental arch at the entrance to the riverside war memorial gardens was built on land donated to Nottingham City Council in 1920 by Sir Jesse Boot, founder of Boot's the Chemists.*

101 *Nottingham's suspension footbridge from Victoria Embankment to Welbeck Road is traditional in design with the span held between twin towers on each bank. It has ironwork from the pre-eminent Andrew Handyside Britannia Foundry of Derby, who also worked on Wilford Bridge and Trent Bridge.*

A triumphal arch at the entrance to the Memorial Gardens bears the apt motto of Nottingham City Council: *Vivit post funera virtus* (Virtue lives after death). Wrought-iron gates of rich turquoise with gold detailing strike a conspicuous contrast with a gleaming white stone surround. Inside, a fine sculpture of Queen Victoria was moved into the grounds from Old Market Square in 1953.

A suspension bridge for pedestrians, its wooden slatted deck vibrating underfoot, leads to Victoria Embankment. Designed to carry a water supply when it was built in 1906, it has signature ironwork from the pre-eminent Andrew Handyside Company.

Nottingham grew up around one of the most important river crossings in England. A bridge was in need of repair in 924. An entry for that year in the Anglo-Saxon Chronicle records: 'This year, before midsummer, went King Edward [Edward the Elder] with an army to Nottingham; and ordered the town to be repaired on the south side of the river, opposite the other, and the bridge over the Trent betwixt the two towns.'

A medieval chronicler described Castle Rock as 'Fortified both by art and nature'. In 1068 William Peveril, one of William the Conqueror's most trusted knights and widely acknowledged as his illegitimate son, chose it as his base from which to command the crossing of the Trent and dominate the surrounding area. Alongside the Saxon borough centred on St Mary's Church, a separate Norman borough was established around the castle. A bank and ditch surrounded both boroughs. Stone ramparts were added in 1267. Remnants of the old town walls were exposed in 1929 when the *Three Crowns* in Upper Parliament Street was demolished to widen the road at the junction with Market Street. Duplication of sheriff and coroner posts survived from the twin borough arrangement until 1835. Peveril's timber keep was rebuilt in stone during the 12th century. Tunnels in the Bunter sandstone beneath gave access to the Trent via the River Leen. Today's baroque palace built in the 1670s is the legacy of William Cavendish, Duke of Newcastle.

The Saxon crossing known as Hethbethe Bridge was rebuilt by Henry II *c*.1156. It first appears as Trent Bridge in records from the mid-1560s. Maintenance was a responsibility shared between the counties of Nottingham, Derby and Leicester. With no single authority in overall control, repairs were neglected. By 1363, Hethbethe Bridge was in such a dilapidated state it had to be closed. A replacement ferry service was authorised for five years and the profits allocated to offset the cost of reconstruction. With their trade affected, Nottingham's burgesses

102 *Crouching beneath Nottingham Castle, its cellars burrowing into Castle Rock,* Ye Olde Trip to Jerusalem *claims to be the oldest inn in England, reputedly founded at the time of the Third Crusade in 1189. Tunnels in the sandstone outcrop once linked the castle to the Trent via the River Leen.*

103 *Nottingham's medieval 'old' Trent Bridge. The structure underwent major refurbishment in 1684 and 1725 but was unable to cope with the demands of increasing traffic and was replaced in 1871.*

decided to take over liability. Various bequests and grants made over the years for the upkeep of the bridge were consolidated into the Bridge Estate and two bridge masters were appointed. A causeway, known as 'Cheney Bridges' because chains prevented it being used except in times of flood, led over marshland from Trent Bridge to a crossing of the River Leen.

Regular dredging of the Trent in Tudor times provided sufficient material to pave the streets of Nottingham at a time when most cities had to contend with muddy, rutted thoroughfares.

King Charles I raised his standard beside St James's Church at the Hollows, now Standard Hill, Nottingham, on 22 August 1642, signalling the start of seven years of armed conflict. At the outbreak of Civil War, Parliamentarian forces moved quickly to fortify Trent Bridge. In 1643, a small Royalist force from Newark entered Nottingham under cover of darkness, forcing the surprised Parliamentarian troops to barricade themselves in the castle and await reinforcements. Although the town was soon recaptured, a Royalist force held out at the bridge for a further 10 days. Loss of the bridge caused such disruption for the resident garrison that, according to Sir George Gresley of Drakelow, one of the Parliamentarian commanders, the Governor of Nottingham declared, 'Unless our soldiers would stay and take the bridge he would quit the castle'.

In addition to regular maintenance, major rebuilding of Nottingham's Trent Bridge proved necessary in 1684 and again in 1725. Despite widening, the bridge was unable to cope with increased traffic that accompanied industrial growth in the 19th century. In 1871, a new iron bridge of three spans, with ornamental cast-iron of high quality from the world famous Britannia Foundry workshops of Andrew Handyside at Derby, opened alongside the stone crossing with its much patched-up arches. Old Trent Bridge was demolished shortly afterwards except for a 14th-century fragment comprising two approach arches on the south bank that now stand in the centre of a small traffic island outside County Hall. Dredging removed the ancient ford upstream of the bridge.

New Trent Bridge was soon having difficulty coping with the volume of traffic crossing the river and was widened further in 1926. A major facelift in 1987 included fresh royal blue and gold paint for the ironwork and colourful detailing for decorative floral motifs. A stonework abutment is marked with a scale showing the height in feet above ordnance datum and the levels reached by floods experienced over the years.

Despite rising concerns about pollution and sewage outfall, the river either side of Trent Bridge was popular with swimmers. In 1857, Nottingham Corporation provided bathers with changing facilities and an attendant.

104 *Two approach arches of a medieval bridge, demolished shortly after Nottingham's new Trent Bridge opened in 1871, remain in the centre of a small traffic island outside County Hall.*

105 *The chimney rising behind Nottingham's Trent Bridge belongs to the pumping station of Trent Water Works, demolished in the early 20th century. Nottingham Corporation was the first in the country to provide mains water at high pressure to reduce the risk of contamination. Supplies were filtered into a reservoir beside the pumping station.*

Nottingham's three rowing clubs – Nottingham and Union Rowing Club, Nottingham Boat Club, and Nottingham Britannia Rowing Club – now compete at the National Water Sports Centre but a traditional Head of the Trent race still takes place, conditions permitting, on the river, starting at Clifton.

Beside Trent Bridge, a small public garden is a quiet riverside haven opposite the towering curve of Rushcliffe Civic Centre and Nottingham Forest Football Club's City Ground. Beyond is Trent Bridge Test and County Cricket Ground. Notts County Football Club is also based close to the river at Meadow Road. When

All Saints Church at Adbolton was demolished in 1746, masonry was recycled to strengthen the wharf-lined banks. Little about the modern riverside gives any clue to Nottingham's days as a busy inland port at the head of the Trent Navigation. Most reminders are restricted to the Nottingham Canal, where old warehouses and the former headquarters of leading canal carriers, Fellows, Morton & Clayton Ltd, have been rejuvenated as offices, pubs and cafes. Nottingham Canal meets the river opposite the City Ground. Downstream is the boathouse of Nottingham Kayak Club and the entrance to the Grantham Canal, closed in 1929 and partly filled in but now undergoing restoration.

Lady Bay Bridge, a flat-decked girder viaduct of two spans, was built as a railway bridge and converted when the line closed in 1969. It stands close to the site of a horse bridge that was swept away by floodwater in 1875. Below Lady Bay Bridge is Nottingham Forest's training ground and the headquarters of Nottingham Sailing Club. Opposite are the dock terminals where cargoes were transferred from narrowboats and shallow draught Upper Trent vessels to keels and other craft for onward shipment.

In the course of travelling 15 miles from Holme Pierrepont to Fiskerton the Trent falls over 20 feet. Consequent strengthening of the current created problems for shipping. Improvements to the Navigation in the 1910s and 1920s, including new locks at Cromwell, Hazelford, Gunthorpe, Stoke Bardolph and Holme Pierrepont, enabled larger vessels to reach Nottingham. As part of ongoing flood protection work, immense sluices replaced a flood lock at Holme Pierrepont in 1952. Five automatically operated steel gates respond to water levels to reduce flood risk.

106   *Nottingham's annual regatta drew large crowds to the riverside. In addition to rowing races, a variety of entertainment was on offer, including a greasy pole challenge that involved most competitors in a ducking. Nottingham International Regatta now takes place at the National Water Sports Centre at Holme Pierrepont.*

107   *In the late 19th and early 20th centuries, steamers ran regular passenger services to Colwick Park from*
these landing stages beside Trent Bridge. In the background is Lady Bay Bridge.

Holme Pierrepont ('Pierrepont' was added to the name in the 13th century when the Manvers family heiress married Henry of Pierrepont Castle, France) is the location for one of six specialist national sports centres. It was developed from a series of pits left by gravel extraction and includes Skylark Nature Reserve. Regatta Lake hosts canoeing, rowing and dragon boat races. Facilities on the rest of the complex include white water rafting, cycling and clay pigeon shooting. Georgian and Victorian wings at Holme Pierrepont Hall flank one of the earliest surviving examples of brick construction in the Trent Valley, a red-brick entrance and south range that date back to an original Tudor courtyard house.

Steamers once ran regularly from landing stages beside Trent Bridge to Colwick Park,

a prime Trentside location and the site of a homestead since before the Norman Conquest. The Milnefleet, an artificial stream that powered a mill mentioned in Domesday Book, disappeared when gravel excavation and the subsequent creation of Colwick Country Park changed the topography. Colwick, along with Wollaton, became part of the City of Nottingham in 1933. A marina is accessible from the river. Two lakes cater for sailing, sail-boarding, model boat enthusiasts and coarse fishing. Hall Pool, largely surrounded by trees, is a nature reserve. Tranquil gardens surround the roofless ruin of 16th-century St John the Baptist Church. Horse racing moved to Colwick from the Forest area of Nottingham in the 1890s. Georgian Colwick Hall, attached to the racecourse, is also a conference centre.

Seven

On the River's Margin Thrive:
The Trent Vale and Newark

After passing under a railway viaduct and smothering tiny Poiser Brook, the river meets the red cliffs that gave Radcliffe on Trent its name. The former wharf is now a riverside residential park. What was a rural farming village has become part of Nottingham's dormitory belt. The Trent Valley Way follows the wooded, sandstone edge with the river grave and glittering below. In the shadow of Gibbet Hill are Stoke Lock and Island. Stoke Wood, planted to provide fuel for river steamers, is now managed for the benefit of wildlife and visitors. A display panel beside the lock provides visitors with historical and environmental information. The

Ferry Boat Inn marks the site of the former passenger crossing.

Curling through the water meadows of the Holmes, the Hams' (from 'hamm' meaning a river bend rather than 'ham' a settlement), and Burton Meadows, the Trent passes Burton Joyce, Bulcote, and Shelford.

Burton Joyce acquired its suffix from the de Jorz family, lords of the manor in the 13th and 14th centuries. St Helen's Church, susceptible to flooding over the years, has some attractive stained glass including bold designs from the London studios of Victorian glasswork artist, Charles Kempe.

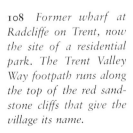

108 *Former wharf at Radcliffe on Trent, now the site of a residential park. The Trent Valley Way footpath runs along the top of the red sandstone cliffs that give the village its name.*

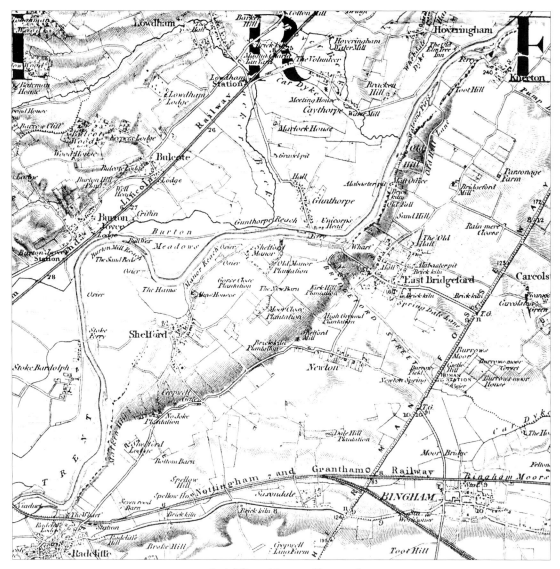

109   *Radcliffe on Trent to Hoveringham.*

Shelford Manor, then the home of Colonel Philip Stanhope, was subjected to a savage assault by Parliamentarian troops during the Civil War. The besiegers under Colonel John Hutchinson had a torrid time, caught in crossfire between the manor and a Royalist detachment stationed in the belfry of St Peter's Church. Once the men in the church had been smoked out, allegedly by lighting a fire in the tower, it was only a matter of time. No quarter was

shown. Stanhope was killed and the house torched. Only 40 men survived of a garrison of two hundred.

A tollbridge at Gunthorpe replaced a ferry in 1875. The iron span was demolished when a modern, toll-free crossing carrying the A6097 opened in 1927, but the tollhouse and remnants of massive stone buttresses can still be seen. Gunthorpe Lock gates were replaced in 1999 using a West African hardwood from forests managed for sustainability. As at Stoke Lock, there is a British Waterways information board. An audio post features an old boatman recounting his experiences.

Cuttle Hill screens East Bridgford from the river. A former wharf is now a marina and a red sandstone cliff shelters a small beach. Dover Beck falls into the river just before Hoveringham. Aggregate extraction has left Gibsmere and Bleasby surrounded by lakes. The Nabbs, a large island, divides the river into two channels. At Hazelford, a barrier protects an L-shaped weir while the main channel takes boats through the lock. On summer weekends Hazelford Ferry provides a service for anglers.

Trent Hills escarpment, tree clad and steep, is a picturesque backdrop clinging to the east bank past Kneeton, Syerston Airfield and East Stoke. Old Hill (252 ft) and Toot Hill (246 ft) are prominent. 'Toot', an Old English word, suggests a lookout point.

Syerston Airfield was one of many bomber stations built in the 1930s amid concerns about military build up in Germany. During the Second World War it was home to a Polish squadron flying Wellington bombers and was briefly manned by Canadian airmen before the Royal Air Force took over regular operations with a fleet of Lancaster aircraft. By the close of the war, Syerston had become a training airfield. Most of the remaining wartime buildings were demolished in 1997.

Before Newark's Nether Lock and Town Lock were built, and afterwards when river levels were low, Fiskerton Wharf was used as a transhipment point where boats bound upriver could unload part of their cargo to reduce draught. A wharfside crane was made necessary when the riverbank was faced with protective steel piles and a slipway removed. Houses line a grassy embankment behind a stone flood protection wall. Fiskerton Mill straddles the tiny River

110   *As a result of weight restrictions and charges (lorries up to six tons were allowed to cross for 2s 6d) Gunthorpe tollbridge was least used of the seven road bridges across the Trent in Nottinghamshire. It was replaced in 1927. Masonry abutments were left in place (inset) when the iron span was removed.*

Greet close to its confluence with the Trent. The monks of Thurgaton Priory owned a mill on this site in the Middle Ages.

Shakespeare ends the action of his Wars of the Roses play, *Richard III*, with Richard's death at Bosworth Field in 1485, neglecting a final act in which the River Trent played a key role. Francis, Lord Lovell, son of John Lovell, Viscount Beaumont and Jane Bardolph of Stoke Bardolph, was King Richard's Lord Chamberlain. Lovell was satirised at the time by William Collingbourne (later executed for

conspiracy) in a poem that begins: 'The Cat [Sir William Catesby] the Rat [Sir Richard Ratcliffe] and Lovell our dog, rule all England under a hog [Richard's emblem was a white boar with gold tusks].'

Catesby and Ratcliffe both died alongside Richard III at the Battle of Bosworth Field. The Yorkist faction, including Francis Lovell, continued to plot against the new king, Henry Tudor, but with Richard's nephew Edward, Earl of Warwick confined in the Tower of London they lacked a credible claimant to the

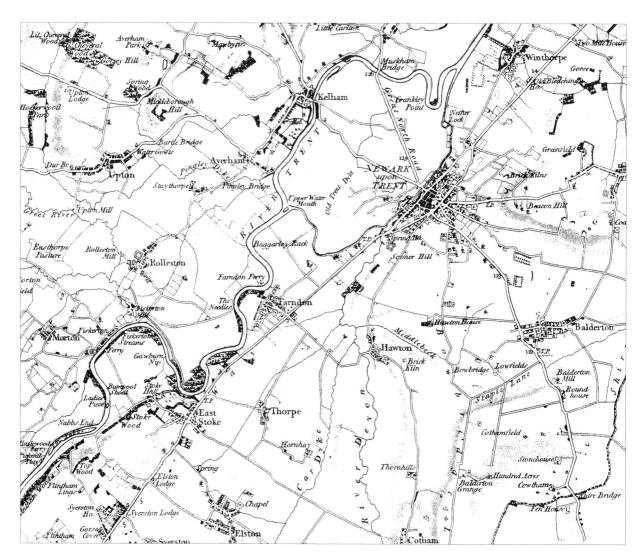

III   *Hazlewood to Winthorpe.*

112 *Site of the ferry crossing at Farndon, once a well-used shortcut for employees of Staythorpe Power Station.*

throne. Ingeniously, they denied that Henry's prisoner was the real Edward and produced Lambert Simnel, a boy of similar age and appearance around whom John de la Pole, Earl of Lincoln, rallied support. A rebel army raised mostly in Ireland and augmented by continental mercenaries landed on the Lancashire coast in June 1487 and headed east across the Pennines hoping to gather support. The River Trent became the focus of a strategic game of cat and mouse. When news reached Henry that his opponents were in York he marched to Nottingham, camping south of the river awaiting news of de la Pole's next move. A number of men suspected of Yorkist sympathies were hung from Trent Bridge as a grim warning to potential spies. The Earl of Lincoln led his forces south. Finding Newark loyal to the King and the town gates barred he forded the Trent at Fiskerton. Henry advanced to a camp between Radcliffe and Shelford, giving him control of crossings as far as Gunthorpe and in a position to cover any attempt by Lincoln to double back north of the river. In the event, the Earl chose to wait for Henry in fields near East Stoke, assembling his forces with the Trent pro-

tecting his rear and the Fosse Way, along which the King's forces were expected, ahead. Fierce fighting followed with neither side gaining an early advantage. As the battle progressed, the superior numbers of the royal forces began to tell. John de la Pole was killed and his troops suffered heavy losses. A deep gulley known as Red Gutter on the hillside above the Trent is said to have been named from the blood of the routed rebels cut down as they retreated. Others, it is claimed, drowned trying to escape across the river. Francis Lovell's body was never found. He may have drowned. It is possible he managed to escape to the family home at Stoke Bardolph and was spirited away to live out the remainder of his life as a fugitive. King Henry moved on to Newark to pray at St Mary's Church and oversee the execution of captives. The child Lambert Simnel was given a job in the royal kitchens and grew up to be royal falconer.

From Fiskerton the river bends through Gawburn Nip, passing Stoke Hall to run parallel with the Fosse Way as it approaches Farndon. 'Nip', meaning a narrow place on the river, is a term peculiar to the Trent.

113 *An example of a working willow 'holt' at Farndon contains a wide variety of species and is of international importance. Willows thrive in wet conditions and osiers were harvested to make baskets and hurdles. Farndon willow holt owes its survival to initial conservation work begun by Lever and Barbara Howitt, now continued by Nottinghamshire Wildlife Trust.*

Farndon ferry operated a convenient shortcut for workers before the closure of Staythorpe Power Station. A new gas-turbine unit is planned to replace its coal-fired predecessor on the site. In 1961, the Central Electricity Generating Board commissioned a sculpture for Staythorpe from Norman Sillman. His striking design of boiler tubes coiled around a turbine, realised in concrete and displayed on the riverside, is entitled 'Power in Trust' after the CEGB motto. Sillman was Head of Sculpture at Nottingham Art College and lived in Nottinghamshire for 18 years. Among Sillman's more familiar designs are the regional variations found on one pound coins.

Farndon is a pretty village with a scatter of elegant Georgian properties clustered around St Peter's Church. Victorian rector Brough Maltby was the guiding force behind substantial restoration and extension of St Peter's. Maltby was responsible for a beautifully carved chancel screen and font cover, and for the acquisition of some vivid windows including a dazzling example from the glassworks of C.E. Kempe in the south wall of the chancel. A circular parish trail leads by the riverside with its yacht club and marina. In a simpler age, the riverbank here was a popular picnic choice, thronged on sunny days with people from Newark and surrounding villages. Farndon Marina was cre-

ated out of a gravel quarry that unexpectedly breached the riverbank, flooding part of the village. A footbridge over the marina entrance was added in 2002.

Nottinghamshire Wildlife Trust has created a 20-acre nature reserve between the river and Wyke Lane. Until recently, Wyke Lane was more familiar locally as 'Coalcart Lane' from the steady stream of traffic collecting coal delivered to the river wharf. As well as flood meadows and arable farmland, the site has a rare surviving willow holt, once a feature of many Trentside villages. Willows thrive in wet conditions. Management by coppicing and pollarding produces fast growing withies or rods that were once harvested to make wicker baskets, fish traps, furniture and hurdles. Demand for containers of all sizes to store and transport goods grew during the Industrial Revolution. Bark was stripped by hand before the introduction of rotating drums that mechanised the process in the late 19th century. A wide variety of species at the Farndon holt includes unique hybrids.

Below Staythorpe the river splits into two channels. Kelham branch slips over Averham Weir and under a railway bridge heading for Averham, Kelham and South Muskham. This arm of the river was a subsidiary stream until 1558 when a cutting diverted the main flow to drive mills owned by the Sutton family of Kelham House. Navigation improvements in 1772 restored the Newark branch as the main channel.

Passing an old windmill to flow beneath the A46, the river collects the River Devon. Newark Rowing Club (founded in 1873) and Newark Marina are conveniently cloistered at the mouth of the Devon. Anglers know different stretches of river from Farndon to Newark as Weir Field, Stone Field, Long Field, Short Field, Hudson's or Kirk's Bay and Devon Mouth.

Kirk's Bay, close to the stump of the former windmill, is one of the sites linked to the mass baptism of early Christian converts, performed by Paulinus in A.D. 627. It was a popular bathing spot a century ago where local children learned to swim. Before swimming baths opened on Sherwood Avenue in 1934, children in Newark progressed through 'test', 'certificate', and 'badge' sections in a stretch of river set aside for public bathing off Tolney Lane.

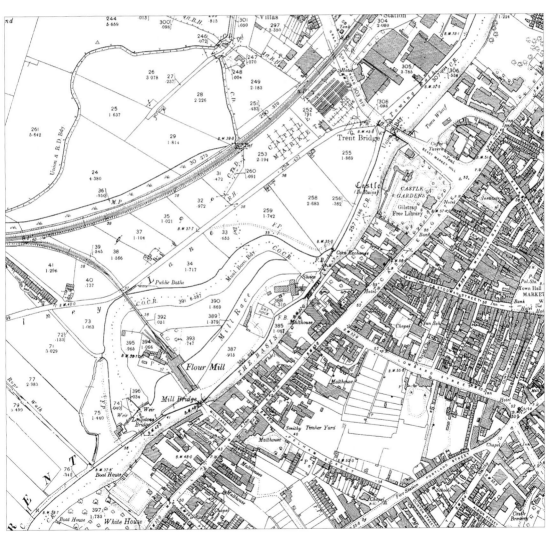

114 *In 1900 Newark: a ropewalk, tannery, timber yard, smithy, several maltings, and the Victorian Corn Exchange cluster around riverside wharves. The 'bathing place', set aside for public swimming off Tolney Lane, was used until Newark's first purpose-built swimming pool (open air) opened in 1934 on Sherwood Avenue.*

115 *Bishop Alexander of Lincoln built Newark Castle and a bridge across the Trent in the 12th century. Royalist forces successfully defended the castle against a series of determined sieges during the Civil War. After the conflict ended much of the building was deliberately destroyed. Newark's present Trent Bridge was built in 1775 and widened in 1848.*

Until recently, there was little evidence of settlement at Newark before the 11th century. Excavations at the castle have now revealed signs of occupation including defensive ditches dating back to the beginning of the Anglo-Saxon period, over five centuries earlier. The manor of Newark became church property in the mid-1050s when Lady Godiva included 'new work', presumably extra fortifications guarding the important river crossing, in her endowment of St Mary's at Stow-in-Lindsey.

In 1135, Henry I was 68 years of age. With no legitimate male heir he was hoping his daughter Matilda would be accepted as ruler after his death. Perhaps anticipating problems when Henry's reign eventually ended, Bishop Alexander of Lincoln used his influential connections to obtain a charter authorising a castle and bridge at Newark. Alexander's 'Uncle' Roger (in fact his father), was Bishop of Salisbury and the King's chief minister. Under the terms of the royal charter, Alexander was allowed to 'Make a ditch and rampart of his fish pond' and 'Divert the Fosseway'. Alexander's fishpond occupied only a narrow strip of land between the Trent and the Fosse Way. Diversion of the highway was a

necessity. The rectangular site dictated the shape of the castle, almost certainly a timber structure. Contemporary chronicler Henry of Huntingdon described the result as 'magnificent', an epithet later applied to Alexander himself. For centuries, Bishop Alexander's bridge was the only crossing downstream of Nottingham.

The early settlement at Newark was in the Northgate area. Alexander laid out a new borough surrounded by a bank and ditch. Stone walls were added in the 14th century. The result of the Bishop's town planning is evident today in the grid of regular streets surrounding Newark's large open market place.

By the end of the 12th century, Newark Castle had been rebuilt in stone. Alterations to strengthen the castle defences continued throughout the medieval period. The river curtain was heightened and crenellated. A watergate gave direct access from the riverside to an undercroft storage area and the castle dungeons. King John visited Newark Castle on a number of occasions and died there in 1216 after being taken ill soon after setting out from Lincoln for Dover, during the struggle with his rebellious barons and their continental ally Louis, Dauphin of France.

Always a convenient sewer and waste disposal channel, chutes from the garderobes or privies in the walls of Newark Castle emptied directly into the river. Slaughterhouses and tanneries were deliberately sited so that butchery waste and fat and hair scraped from hides could be tossed in and carried downstream.

During the Civil War, Newark was recognised as the 'Key to the North', in a pivotal position linking the Royalist headquarters at Oxford and an army under William Cavendish, 1st Duke of Newcastle, based in Yorkshire. Millgate and Northgate were brought within fortifications that enabled the town to withstand three long sieges. The resilience of its 5,000-strong garrison helped sustain the King's cause and a guerrilla campaign continued to inspire the Royalist cause as the first act of the conflict drew to a conclusion. On New Year's Day, 1646 a small force of Cavaliers slipped by their besiegers in the night and launched a hit-and-run raid on the Parliamentarian field headquarters at East Stoke, capturing provisions and taking more than one hundred captives. Newark remained unvanquished until the end, only surrendering on the King's direct orders on 8 May 1646, three days after Charles had given himself up to a Scots Army at Southwell. The garrison marched out undefeated with honour

intact. Within days Newark Castle was largely dismantled to prevent its being re-occupied and used defensively in the future. One of the men employed on demolition, Richard Thorneton of Collingham, was killed by falling masonry. A survey of 1649 described it as 'So ruined that it will never be made habitable, having nothing left but ruinous pieces of walls'. An earthwork known as the 'Queen's Sconce', one of several redoubts and gun batteries built to guard Newark from the south, survives today and is the best preserved example of a Civil War gun battery in the country.

Millgate was prone to flooding before canalisation of the river largely solved the problem. Commercial development began in the Middle Ages with mills, tanneries and other businesses along the riverside. Between 1772 and the mid-19th century river traffic boomed and Newark expanded. Breweries, maltings, cooperages, timber yards, coal depots, and warehouses lined the town's wharves. Millgate grew into a lively area. As trade on the Trent declined the gravitational centre of industry in Newark shifted. After a century of dereliction Millgate was run down, its future in the balance. Long-term regeneration, begun in the late 1960s, focused on retaining the dockland flavour. The result is a now a fashionable mix

116 *Steam tug approaching Trent Bridge at Newark, c.1900.*

117 *The former Trent Navigation Company warehouse at Newark, now a bar and restaurant. Moored in the foreground is the British Waterways tug* Friar Tuck.

118 *Bronze otters by sculptor Judith Bluck enhance a quiet green space at Weighbridge Wharf, Newark.*

of renovated residential and business premises with the feel and character of a village. Modest cottages and small Georgian Houses cluster around courtyards linked by cobbled passageways perfectly evoking Millgate's Trentside heritage. Museum Yard was formerly Oil Mill Yard, home to a seed crushing mill that now houses a folk museum. But Millgate is not a fossilised museum piece. Leisure craft and gravel barges keep Town Lock busy. New businesses, bars and eateries contribute to a spirited atmosphere. The former Trent Navigation Company warehouse is now a waterfront inn. Pints are still pulled at the *Watermill*, first licensed in 1794. As a tribute to those who contributed to the revival of Millgate, Newark and Sherwood District Council commissioned two bronze otters from sculptor Judith Bluck to grace a secluded green space by the river at Weighbridge Wharf.

Newark's bridges, linked by a riverside walk, reflect the town's close relationship with the Trent. Fiddler's Elbow Bridge, more usually shortened to 'the Elbow', was commissioned by the Trent Navigation Company to carry the towpath. A cranked arch of 90 feet, stunningly *avant-garde* when it opened in 1915, was among the first bridges made of reinforced concrete. Countless wet and gritty towropes have scored deep grooves in the railings beneath.

A steel footbridge of three arches crosses the entrance to Kings Marina, home to a wide variety of craft since it opened in 2001. Jubilee Bridge, suspended between 60 ft tall steel masts anchored to the floodplain, opened in 2002 linking Cow Lane with the towpath.

Bishop Alexander's bridge was rebuilt in timber in 1461. The remit included 'Mighty stonework for the defence of the same' at each end of the bridge, a clue that gatehouses once guarded the approaches. The Great North Road marches across the floodplain to South

Muskham on a series of brick arches. John Smeaton, the engineer who trained William Jessop, carried out the work in 1770. Newark's Trent Bridge replaced the medieval bridge in 1775. Built of brick with stone dressing, it was widened in 1848. Ornamental lamp standards and iron railings were added at the same time. A line in the stonework marks the height reached by floodwater in 1875. For some reason, other floods were not recorded. The two-storey former tollhouse still stands in the shadow of the castle on Beast Market Hill. Livestock sales once took place in this broad thoroughfare next to the bridge.

Backwater Bridge, an iron and concrete footbridge from Riverside Park, replaced a wooden haling bridge taking the towpath over the river to Town Lock, in the 1950s. Mill Bridge, leading to British Waterways' workshops and dry dock on what is familiarly known as 'Bob's' or 'Parnham's' Island, is another modern concrete construction, replacement for a hump-backed

119 Humber Trader *heading upriver at Newark with Jubilee Bridge in the background. The bridge, designed locally by Macarthy Hughes International Ltd for Newark and Sherwood District Council, opened in 2002.*

120 *Longstone Bridge, 246 ft long and three feet wide, replaced a wooden bridge carrying the towpath across a weir in the early 19th century.*

121 *A watergate at Newark Castle gave direct access to a landing stage. In the 1470s, when the ornate two-storey oriel window above the watergate was added to light the Great Hall, the river lapped against the curtain wall.*

brick bridge. Parnham's Mill, originally built for spinning cotton in 1790, was destroyed by fire in 1965. The water-powered mill provided employment for many of the poorest families of Newark, including children from the workhouse, but had a relatively short productive life. In the early 1820s it was converted as a flour mill. Longstone Bridge, built in the early 19th century by Newark Navigation Commissioners, carries the towpath on seven arches above the weir where Town Lock and the millrace divert from the main channel. When towing with horses ended, the parapets were raised for safety. Beside the weir are the remains of a sawmill.

Castlegate, dominated by the former Victorian Corn Exchange backing on to the river and the Arts and Crafts style Gilstrap Centre housing the tourist information office, is elsewhere lined with elegant Georgian townhouses. The Market Place is also principally Georgian. Three former coaching inns look out onto the cobbled square. The old town water pump stands in a corner beside a post where bulls were once tethered and baited by dogs. Castle Gardens, first laid out in 1889, had a major make-over for the millennium. Gatehouse, west wall and the sheer river curtain of the castle ruins combine in an impressive testament to former glory. Two distinct types of stone give a chequered effect. Towers at the north-west corner and in the centre of the wall have an angled profile to provide a wide field of vision along the river. Next to the south-west tower a section of crenellated parapet survives. Behind a two-storey oriel window displaying the arms of Thomas Rotherham, Bishop of Lincoln, was the Great Hall remodelled by Rotherham in the 1470s. Beneath the oriel is the watergate. In the 15th century when the river lapped the curtain wall there would have been a wooden landing stage outside.

Beneath the south-west tower is Cuckstool Wharf. In past times, women found guilty of minor disturbances of the peace risked being strapped to a chair or 'cucking stool', dunked in the river and put on public display. Newark's fledgling Corporation (the town was incorporated in 1549) confirmed a local by-law stating, 'If any woman shall scold or disquiet her neighbours she shall be punished upon the cuckstool.' This quaint deterrent and no doubt popular spectator sport continued until the beginning of the 19th century.

Below Newark's Trent Bridge, former maltings have been converted to provide residential apartments and office accommodation. Kiln Warehouse, built as a malting in 1870, is one of the oldest concrete buildings in England.

As the river passes Northgate it flushes Goat Stream, now culverted beneath Queen's Road and Sleaford Road.

The Midland Railway Company viaduct, cast at Andrew Handyside's Derby foundry, crosses alongside the A46 Newark bypass south-west of Nether Lock. A little further on, Newark Dyke Bridge carries the East Coast main line across the river between large 'bowstring' girders. Two separate branches of the river embrace British Sugar's Newark beet factory before converging into a single channel once more at Crankley Point. Downstream, the A1 trunk road spans the stretch of river known as Winthorpe Rack ('rack' denoting shallows).

Medieval timber bridges at South Muskham and Kelham were destroyed in the Civil War. A temporary crossing using boats lashed together was put in place at Kelham by Parliamentarian forces. Robert Manners Sutton, 1st Lord Lexington of Kelham House, was a staunch Royalist. At the end of the conflict, with his estates sequestered and deeply in debt, he was

122 Eskdale *passing Kiln Warehouse, Newark. The former malting, now converted into offices and riverside apartments, was one of the earliest concrete buildings in the country.*

123   Nineteenth-century Kelham Hall is the third house to occupy the site. For many years the main arm of the river went around Newark, by Averham, Kelham and South Muskham. The cutting of Newark Dyke in 1772 restored the shipping route through the town.

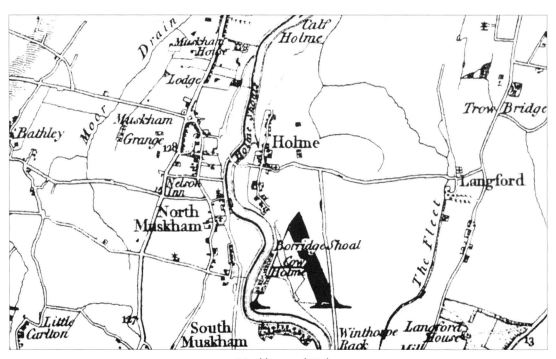

124   Muskham and Holme.

125 *Seen from the site of the former ferry crossing, the cottages of Holme and the modest spire of early-Tudor St Giles's Church rise from behind a curving protective bank. A 15th-century flood changed the course of the Trent overnight, dividing the villages of Holme and North Muskham.*

in no position to pay for a replacement and in any case disputed liability given the deliberate destruction of the old bridge. It was some years later, after restoration of the monarchy and an award of compensation for losses during the Civil War, that a new wooden bridge was erected under pressure from an order issued at Nottingham quarter sessions. Around the same time, Kelham House was rebuilt as Kelham Hall and the opportunity taken to build the new crossing downstream, diverting the Newark to Southwell road away from the grounds of the new mansion. By 1849 the bridge was in a dangerous condition. Again it took a court order to secure a replacement, this time with an iron frame and stone abutments. It did not last long. The winter of 1854/5 was severe. In a prolonged cold spell the river froze. Ice, thick enough for cricket matches to be played on the surface, formed. Sheep roasts were held on the river at Fiskerton. In the spring thaw huge blocks of ice swept downstream on the swollen river. A slab weighing several tons crashed through the iron pilings of Kelham's new bridge causing it to collapse. Maintenance of its replacement, a more substantial structure

of five segmental arches in brick and stone built in 1856, became the responsibility of the County. It was renovated and strengthened in 1988.

The Trent has not always divided North Muskham and Holme. In Tudor times, when two shallow fords were wide enough to accommodate up to forty horses abreast, the river changed its course, possibly overnight, and the old channel subsequently dried up. At the end of Ferry Lane in North Muskham a few wooden jetties and a pontoon extend from the bank. Across the river, red-tiled cottages and the modest spire of Holme church rise behind a curving floodbank. Little more than a generation ago, before a school was built at Holme, children from the village crossed on the ferry to attend classes in North Muskham.

The last sturgeon recorded in the Trent, 8½ ft long and weighing 250 lb, was caught near Holme in 1902. Although once more common, sturgeon has always been exotic enough to attract attention. A large specimen 'captured' at Castle Donington in 1255 was sufficiently noteworthy to warrant a mention in the *Annals of Burton Abbey*.

126 *The last sturgeon recorded in the Trent was caught in 1902. It weighed 250 lb.*

There are other testimonials to the East Midlands wool trade but none more beautiful than tiny St Giles's Church at Holme, enlarged and reworked by John Barton shortly before his death in 1491. Originally from Lancashire, Barton was a wool merchant operating in Calais who married Isabella Gernon, member of a wealthy Nottinghamshire family descended from the Earls of Chester. Barton made a huge fortune exporting wool to France from the wharves of Newark. According to Nottinghamshire historian, Dr Robert Thoroton, writing in 1677, a window of Barton's house at Holme was inscribed: 'I thanke God, and ever shall, It is the shepe hath payed for all.'

Clearly in later life he turned his thoughts to the need for salvation. His will instructed son Ralph to organise a priest to sing mass for his soul in the Lady Chapel at St Giles's after his death. An unusually large porch has an upstairs room, possibly intended as accommodation for the mass priest. For many years it was known as Nan Scott's Chamber after a woman said to have sought refuge from an outbreak of plague in the 17th century. Barely touched by time, St Giles's is a magnificent early Tudor church. Above the entrance to the porch is a frieze of seven finely carved shields. In the centre, flanked by various family quarterings and impalings, the arms of the Merchants of the Staple of Calais (falcon, dolphins and sheep) sit alongside those of the Wool Merchants (bales of wool). Inside the Lady Chapel, a riot of vigorous and vividly realised eagles, dogs, salamanders, poppyheads, and angelic forms decorate bench ends.

Eight

Surely to the Sea:
Cromwell to Gainsborough and Trent Falls

Cromwell Lock is the largest inland tidal lock. Before it was built, tidal influence, although small, was discernible as far as Collingham and Newark. A stone inscribed 1884 marks the remains of ancient bridge piers discovered in 1792 and removed during improvements to the Navigation. Thought at the time to be Roman, the bridge is now known to date from the eighth century. The volume of water pouring over the large weir creates a constant thundering rumble and once posed a serious hazard. A memorial remembers 10 soldiers of the Royal Engineers Parachute Squadron who lost their lives in a tragic accident during a night exercise in 1975. There were further catastrophes before doubts about the practicability of a barrier with the potential to collect debris were overcome and a string of warning buoys set in place.

From Cromwell, the character of the river changes. It is almost as if the river breathes. The rhythmic ebb and flow is not a tug-of-war but a dance in which the partners take turns to lead. Boaters must be mindful of tidal fluctuations when planning journeys and observe the navigation markers warning of shallows and submerged islands. Leisure vessels need to be aware of commercial craft and their crews familiar with warning sounds and signals. Equipment should be checked to ensure it is in full working order and charts are up to date. Tidal locks require a careful approach and are operated by lock keepers. Non-tidal locks can be self-operated and are fitted with traffic lights.

When the lock keeper is not on duty an amber light is displayed. When the lock keeper is on duty, a red light means stop while the lock is set. Green signifies 'Proceed'.

Mineral quarries stretch from Collingham to South Clifton. Conveyors can be moved and linked to carry aggregate from excavation sites direct to wharves at Besthorpe, Girton, Carlton, Sutton, and elsewhere for loading onto barges. Restoration of former gravel workings managed by Nottinghamshire Wildlife Trust has resulted in Besthorpe Nature Reserve, currently occupying 150 acres and with plans to expand. An alluvial meadow area south of Trent Lane is a designated Site of Special Scientific Interest (SSSI). Great burnet with its deep red flowers, and pepper saxifrage (properly an umbellifer not a pepper or a saxifrage) are among the wildflower species found here. Herons and cormorants nest at Mons Pool. Shingle areas provide habitat for little ringed plover and other wading birds. At Spalford Warren Nature Reserve, another site with SSSI status, Nottinghamshire Wildlife Trust is clearing Forestry Commission conifers to restore a rare example of an inland grassheath to its natural state.

Highest point along the flat valley floor is Clifton Hill, just 75 ft above sea level. The river curves and loops around areas of marshland in sweeping meanders. Villages on both banks stand behind the immediate floodplain. A line in the masonry of All Saints Church at Collingham records the height reached by

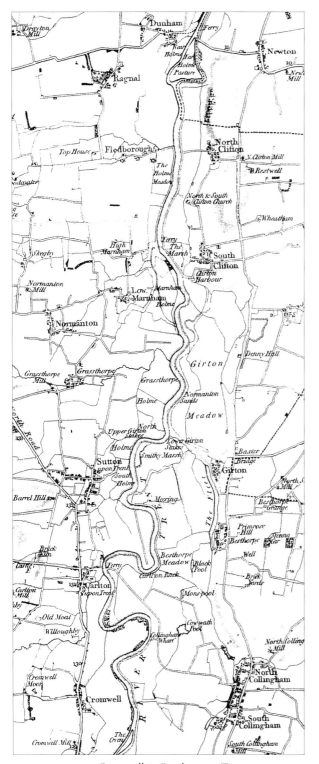

127 *Cromwell to Dunham on Trent.*

floodwater in February 1795, five feet above road level.

Between the skeletal bulk of High Marnham Power Station, now decommissioned as a generating site, and the red-tile pyramid cap of St Gregory's at Fledborough, no longer used for Sunday worship, an equally redundant railway strides across the valley on 39 arches. A further 10 arches complete the viaduct on the eastern bank. In 1728, the Reverend William Sweetapple of Fledborough was deputed to issue marriage licences. Between then and the 1753 Marriage Act that made residency a compulsory requirement, the minister ran a lucrative sideline, marrying runaway couples seeking a more accessible alternative to Gretna Green.

At Dunham on Trent, a girder bridge carries twin pipes across the river. Boreholes at Elkesley near Worksop were tapped to supply Lincoln with clean, fresh water following a typhoid epidemic in 1911. The bridge was completed the following year. Immediately downstream, Dunham's tollbridge was the result of concerted action by local farmers seeking a convenient crossing to deliver produce and livestock to market. An Act of Parliament was obtained in 1830. An issue of £50 shares provided the funds and a cast-iron structure was in place by 1832. It is still privately owned. Below the tollbridge, a straight stretch of river known as Dunham Rack flows strongly between floodbanks.

Laneham, with its ford was an important crossing. A Saxon church was rebuilt in Norman style after the Conquest. A weatherworn plain oak door, one of just a handful of Norman doors to survive in England (there is another Trentside at St Mary Magdalene, Attenborough) has only recently been replaced and is now propped against the wall inside the church at the rear of the nave. The walls of the ringing chamber in the tower of St Peter ad Vincula are decorated with crudely painted circles containing letters and dates ranging from 1813 to 1840. Couples marrying in the church paid the bell ringers to inscribe their initials inside a 'cheese' or 'wedding ring' on the walls of the bell tower.

128 *A girder bridge carrying a water pipeline crosses the river close to the road tollbridge at Dunham on Trent.*

129 *For good luck, couples marrying at St Peter ad Vincula, Church Laneham in the early 19th century gave either five shillings or a sage cheese to the bell ringers in return for having their initials inscribed inside a 'cheese' or 'wedding ring' painted on the bell tower walls.*

The fee was traditionally five shillings or a sage cheese. In the Middle Ages, the Archbishops of York had a palace at Laneham, probably on the site now occupied by Manor Farm. In the first half of the 13th century, Archbishop Gray, builder of Southwell Minster's magnificent quire, signed more than forty official documents from Laneham and may have been the inspiration behind the elegant north arcade at

St Peter's. An oak chest incised with sunflower roundels and a fragment of glass showing the Virgin Mary are from the same period.

The *Ferry Boat Inn* at Church Laneham stands by a tiny village green from where a short track leads to the riverside. A ferry scene on the inn sign actually shows East Stockwith.

With the development of Rampton Quarry in the early 1980s, aggregate was loaded onto

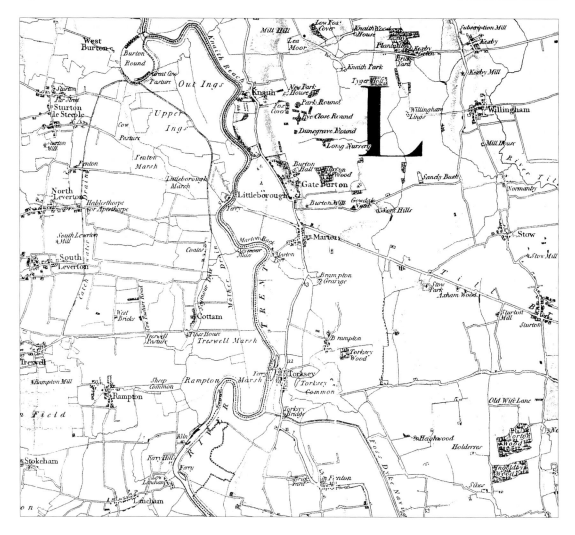

130 *Laneham to West Burton.*

131 *A short cut lined with mooring pontoons links the Trent to the Fossdyke via a double-gated sea-lock (inset). Cottam Power Station is in the background.*

barges below Laneham. Heading for Torksey, the river performs a double loop as it passes Laughterton Marsh, a low-lying area criss-crossed by drainage ditches.

A short side channel leads to Torksey Lock and the Fossdyke. Floating pontoons provide overnight moorings for passing craft. To deal with fluctuating water levels, tidal or sea locks have paired gates that prevent a high tide flooding into the connecting waterway, and a second set to stop water draining out as the tide ebbs. A visitor interpretation centre opened at Torksey Lock in 2004.

Damply clamped to the riverside, the west facade of Torksey Castle rises bleak and gaunt, all that remains of a three-storey mansion built by Sir Robert Jermyn in the 1560s. Archaeological investigation has shown that the site was occupied from Torksey's Saxon glory days when wharves and buildings lined the entrance to the Fossdyke.

Torksey had declined as a port by 1300, overtaken by its neighbour Gainsborough. The Fossdyke proved difficult to maintain and by the 17th century was only passable with difficulty. Lincoln Corporation tinkered with piecemeal improvements before eventually leasing the waterway to Richard Ellison in 1740. Four years of dredging and scouring the channel paid off. By the close of the 18th century the Ellison family had become wealthy on the proceeds.

Opposite Torksey, Cottam Power Station's eight cooling towers stand in two regimented ranks aligned north to south. If plans to open up a disused railway bridge to walkers are successful, it will give access from Torksey to the Trent Valley Way footpath.

Trent Port Road and Littleborough Lane link Marton to the riverside. In the early part of the 19th century Richard Furley's boats left daily bound for Lincoln via the Fossdyke, Newark, Nottingham and Shardlow. An anchor, dredged from the riverbed, was set up outside St Margaret of Antioch Church in 2003, a visible reminder of Marton's Trentside heritage. Of Trent Port with its cluster of warehouses nothing now

132 *The west façade is all that remains of a three-storey Tudor mansion known as Torksey Castle built by Sir Robert Jermyn.*

133 *A typical Admiralty pattern anchor dredged from the river nearby and put on display outside the church of St Margaret of Antioch is an appropriate symbol of Marton's Trentside heritage. Early Norman masonry is visible in the church tower.*

remains except for a converted windmill built in 1799. Partially dismantled in 1926, the truncated tower looks out over the river from the summit of a low cliff. A grindstone with characteristic harp-shaped grooves is set in the grass outside. At first glance, the riverbank below appears swathed with nettle, cow parsley and burdock but it also contains water figwort, woundwort and other delicate surprises.

Littleborough Lane, the route followed by Roman legions two thousand years ago, and where King Harold and his army marched on their way to that fateful history-changing engagement at Hastings, ends expectantly opposite Littleborough, no longer linked by ford or ferry.

The landscaped grounds of Gate Burton Hall run down to the Trent where a delightfully quirky stone temple known as the Chateau, built as a weekend retreat in 1747, stands atop a grassy knoll. Here, in the shadow of West Burton Power Station, the river winds in a large meander from Knaith around Lea Marsh. West Burton village dwindled and disappeared around

134   *A riverside windmill, built in 1799 when Trent Port at Marton was a busy wharf, was partially dismantled in 1926. A grindstone is set in the grass outside.*

1800. Only the platforms of some 14 houses and a sunken roadway survive. St Helen's Church was demolished in 1885.

A succession of water meadows known by the Old English term 'ing' extend north from Littleborough, past West Burton towards Beckingham. Subject to regular flooding that kept them relatively frost free and well-fertilised, the pastures of Upper Ings, Out Ings, and Bole Ings produced lush early grass, important to the local agricultural economy until the beginning of the 19th century. Rounding a hairpin bend known as Stoney Bight, the river approaches Gainsborough.

Managed willow beds on Beckingham Marshes supported a thriving industry until the 1930s. The marshes were drained and ploughed in the 1960s, changing the character of the land. Since then, subterranean gas and oil fields have been developed commercially. Now, the Royal Society for the Protection of Birds has established a nature reserve and the area is being actively managed in conjunction with local farmers. The aim is to restore the habitat as a grazing marsh that will provide vital flood protection for Gainsborough while encouraging a diverse array of wetland wildlife including water voles, lapwing, redshank and snipe.

A section of Pigot and Co.'s *National Commercial Directory* for 1830 described Gainsborough in the following terms:

> It consists principally of one long street, parallel with the river, which is navigable to this place for vessels of 150 tons burden. By means of this stream, which unites with the Humber river, and the Readley and Chesterfield canals, it carries on a considerable trade in corn and other commodities, to and from the coast, and also participates with Hull in the trade to the Baltic; and so much has the trade increased of late years, that a custom-house has been established. There are several very respectable concerns in the glass and lead trade; those of Messrs. Furley and Co. Flower & Co. and Mr George Barley, being very extensive; the former house having also large rope works. Ship building is a branch here of some consequence; the yards of Messrs. Furley & Co. and Mr Henry Smith being the principal ones.

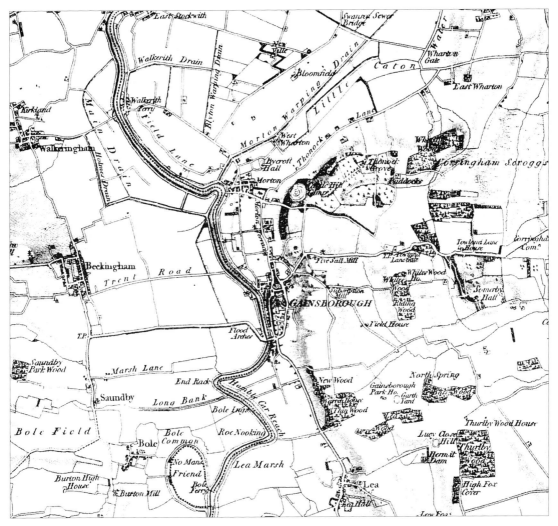

135   *Lea to East Stockwith.*

Signs of Gainsborough's glory days as a port and trading centre with a proud engineering heritage are reflected in the splendid timber-framed Old Hall, the grandeur of All Saints Church, a range of handsome Georgian properties and solid industrial buildings.

A bridge across the Trent at Gainsborough, mentioned in a royal charter of 1141, had disappeared by the end of the 13th century and the site has never been identified. During the Civil War a bridge of boats was set in place as a temporary measure. When Gainsborough's Trent Bridge opened fully in 1791 it was the only

crossing between Newark and the Humber Estuary. Local architect and builder William Weston designed the solidly handsome bridge and its tollhouses. The cost of using the 'Gateway to Gainsborough' was the same as for the ferry it replaced. Charges were necessary but unpopular. Freedom from toll in 1932 was a cause for celebration. The former tollgates are now on riverside display beside Whittons Gardens. The bridge was widened in 1964.

A prime candidate for the original of Dorlcote Mill, where the Tulliver family lived in a 'Trimly-kept, comfortable dwelling-house' in

136 *Gainsborough's triple-arched Trent Bridge was built between 1787-91 of York stone. Twin tollhouses were constructed at the same time. The 68-mile towpath from Shardlow to Gainsborough passed beneath the bridge on a timber jetty.*

137 *Celia, one of Gainsborough United Steam Packet Company's fleet of paddle steamers, passing Mercer's (also known at various times as 'Riverside' or 'Union') Mill at Gainsborough around 1910. The tower mill was one of a number of candidates locally that may have inspired the fictional 'Mill on the Floss', immortalised in George Eliot's popular Victorian novel.*

George Eliot's *Mill on the Floss*, stood near Trent Bridge. Gainsborough, 'Its aged, fluted red roofs and the broad gables of its wharves between the low wooded hill and the river brink' was transmuted into 'St Ogg's', Morton into 'Tofton', and the Trent into the 'Floss' in the popular Victorian novel.

Sir Thomas Burgh rebuilt Old Hall around 1480, after supporters of the Lancastrian cause set fire to his mansion during the Wars of the Roses. Richard III rewarded his loyalty by staying in 1483. Sir William Hickman bought the house in 1596 and the property stayed with descendants of his family until it was given to the nation in 1970. Hickman, a London businessman, used his connections in the capital to broker distribution deals with a number of London merchants. As a result, Gainsborough became the main port of entry for London freight where it was transhipped for carriage inland on smaller vessels. As trade grew an annual three-day market was extended to nine days and a second market, also of nine days, was authorised.

138 *Gainsborough Old Hall, one of the best-preserved timber-framed medieval manors in the country, originally built c.1460 by Sir Thomas Burgh. It was bought by London merchant, William Hickman, in 1596 and remained in the family until given to the nation in 1970. Hickman used his business connections to expand shipping at Gainsborough.*

139 *In the 17th century, Gainsborough Wharf became the main port of entry for goods shipped from London.*

140 *Part of the waterfront at Gainsborough, decayed and derelict by the 1980s, transformed by a flood defence barrier (completed in 2000) and imaginative renovation of riverside buildings.*

The eight-pinnacled medieval tower of All Saints was retained when the parish church was rebuilt in fine classic style between 1736-44 using London's St Martin-in-the-Fields and Derby's All Saints Cathedral as design models.

After decades of decline and neglect Gainsborough has re-engaged with its riverside. New flood defences from Corporation Yard beside Trent Bridge, past the former barley store of Sandars Maltings, to Chapel Staith were completed in 2000. Since then, this stretch of the waterfront has been thoughtfully revitalised. Derelict industrial buildings have been refurbished and Whittons Mill converted into a mix of luxury apartments and flats for the elderly.

Creative sculpture, seating, audio portholes, and landscaping, all inspired by the River Trent,

add a lively dimension to the new Riverside Walk. At night, the twin tollhouses on Trent Bridge are imaginatively lit. A floating pontoon at Gleadell's Wharf provides 'pay and display' mooring for leisure craft. Plans for a marina are at an advanced stage.

On the opposite bank is an area of overgrown scrubland known as Dog Island. Buried here are the remnants of a port complex that grew up around Beckingham in the 19th century to avoid tolls and wharfage charged at the townside wharves of Gainsborough. Buildings on Dog Island were destroyed by fire in 1873. Shipping was in decline and the site was subsequently abandoned. Dog Island is now protected as a Scheduled Ancient Monument.

North of Gainsborough, the river bends sharply at Morton Corner, once a busy shipping wharf where smuggling was a profitable sideline. A secret passage leading from Morton Mill to a house in Front Street was used to deliver contraband brandy to the *Sailor Boy Inn*. Downstream of the village a warping drain empties through a sluicegate at a spot known to generations of local children as 'Smugglers Cove'.

Flanked by floodbanks, the river flows past Walkerith heading for East and West Stockwith. East Stockwith's former quay is lined with houses and the Victorian church of St Peter stands close to the river. A ferry ran between East and West Stockwith until declining trade and problems with licence renewal forced closure in 1952.

A tidal lock marks the entrance to West Stockwith Basin. Floodgates form a barrier across the mouth of the River Idle. Backers of the Chesterfield Canal argued for some time over the route of the cutting. The cost and challenge of tunnelling through Castle Hill, east of

Retford, eventually swung the balance away from a terminal at Gainsborough. It was a decision that turned the wharf at West Stockwith into a flourishing port with a population over five thousand. Its river-linked prosperity is reflected in tall, spacious houses built by merchants and ship owners. St Mary's Church was built in 1722, of red brick in keeping with the rest of the village, out of the estate of William Huntington, a shipbuilder or 'ship carpenter' as he styled his craft. West Stockwith Basin once boasted five boatyards. It is now home to two sailing clubs and is a popular mooring site for pleasure craft. Around the basin, wavy Baroque silhouettes of Dutch-style gables recall the influence of the Low Countries, prevalent in the Isle of Axholme.

The Isle of Axholme, briefly transferred to Humberside after the local government boundary reforms of 1974, is once more part

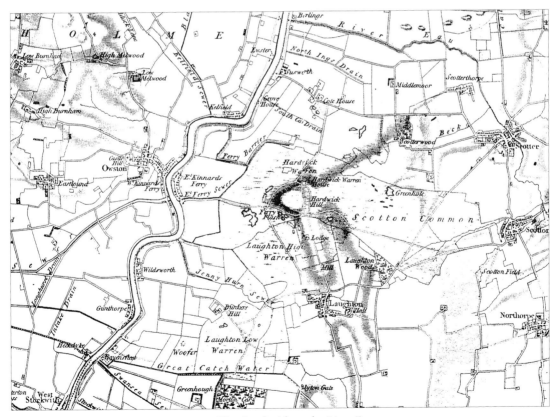

141   *West Stockwith to the River Eau.*

of Lincolnshire. Although not strictly an island it was largely surrounded by water until the 17th century. Low lying and reliant on drainage to control the constant threat of flood, it remains a unique area with a strong sense of identity. In the Middle Ages, Axholme was under the lordship of the Mowbray family, among the few feudal masters who allowed tenants to control fishing and ferry rights. Large tracts of marsh were reclaimed by drainage schemes implemented in the 1620s and the land sold off for farming. It was an unpopular move with locals who had adapted to working with the regular floods that enriched the land and stood to lose long-held common rights. Water levels were lowered to a point where ferries could no

longer operate into South Yorkshire from the east of the Isle, but land remained too water-logged for easy travel overland. The River Trent became a lifeline and Owston Ferry developed as Axholme's main port, handling most of the goods in and out of the Isle before the Axholme Light Railway was built in the early years of the 20th century. Along the riverbank are three converted windmills. Sails last turned in the 1920s and were removed shortly afterwards. Owston Ferry's Old Smithy on High Street, little changed since it closed for business in 1958, now houses a museum and heritage centre. St Martin's Church occupies what would have been the bailey of the Mowbrays' typically Norman motte and bailey castle, lost to Henry II in 1174.

142 *A converted tower windmill on the riverside south of Owston Ferry. When it was operational from the early 19th century until c.1920, the distinctive ogee-shaped cap could be rotated, positioning four sails to catch the prevailing wind and drive grindstones set on each of the three lower storeys.*

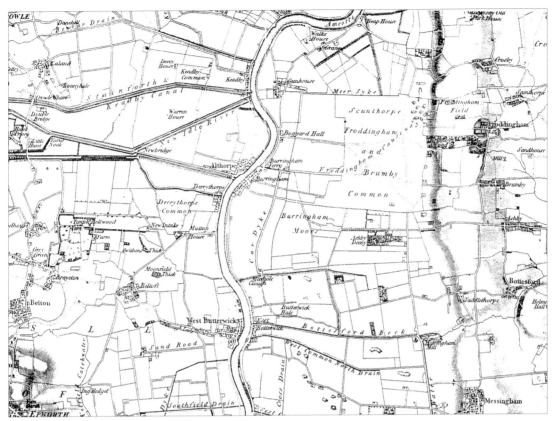

143   *Butterwick to Keadby. In the first half of the 19th century, Ashby, Brumby, Cosby and Frod[d]ingham were separate small villages not yet subsumed into Scunthorpe.*

144   *King George V road and rail bridge at Keadby opened in 1916. A 190 ft swinging section was raised using a counterpoise mechanism to allow sailing barges to pass without lowering their masts. Problems with the machinery and a decline in shipping led to a decision in 1958 to fix the lifting arm permanently.*

145 *Barges and keels queue at Keadby landing stage, c.1930. Tugs and other boats pass in the main channel.*

Founder of Methodism John Wesley was born and grew up with his brother Charles at the Old Rectory, Epworth.

Beyond East Ferry, the River Eau surrenders to the Trent. The hills of Scotton Common, cloaked in a plantation of trees, rise incongruously in the flat landscape. The houses of East and West Butterwick straggle either side of the river behind their floodbanks. At East Butterwick the waters of Bottesford Beck, once the Trent's most polluted tributary, slough into the river upstream of a reinforced concrete span carrying the M180.

A group of quiet villages that included Ashby, Brumby, Crosby and Frodingham grew into Scunthorpe Town, a centre for steel production, after the discovery of rich ironstone deposits in the middle of the 19th century. Scunthorpe is now home to a diverse range of manufacturing industries.

Great Central Railways built the King George V road and rail bridge at Keadby in 1916 to replace an earlier model constructed by South Yorkshire Railway and the River Don Company in the 1860s. A 190 ft long lifting arm was raised to allow river traffic to pass. Problems with the mechanism and a decline in the amount of shipping led to a decision to fix the swing section in 1958. In the years that followed, carriage of aggregates increased the number and size of boats on the Navigation. Vessels had to be fitted with retractable wheelhouses in order to negotiate the bridge.

Under the shadow of Keadby Power Station, wharves at Althorpe and Gunness face each other. The Three Rivers drainage channels, natural watercourses first re-engineered by Cornelius Vermuyden in the 17th century, empty and the Stainforth and Keadby Canal locks into the river. Tricky currents make the lock keeper's advice a prudent step before attempting to negotiate the tidal lock. In 1986, New Wharf opened alongside the canal entrance.

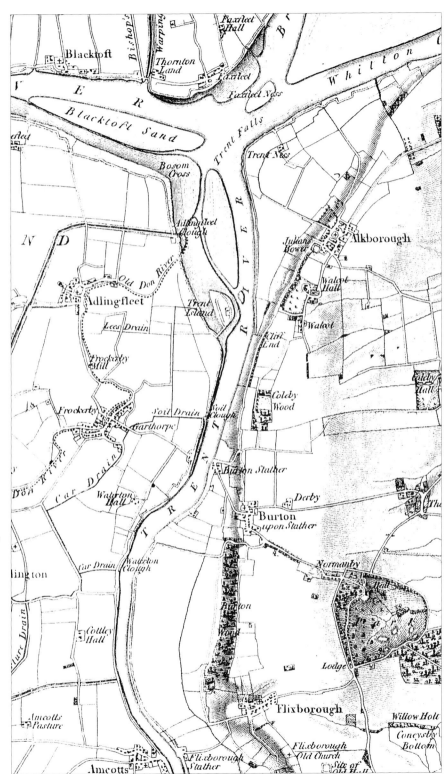

146 *Flixborough to Trent Falls.*

Grove Wharf and its smaller neighbour, Neap House Wharf, are convenient quays for Flixborough and the industrial estates around Scunthorpe. The village of Flixborough is set back from the river on a finger of higher ground that stretches through Burton Wood to enfold Burton Stather and touch Alkborough. Tiny All Saints Church is built of warm brown sandstone with a wooden bell turret. On Saturday, 1 June 1974, a leak of cyclohexane at the Nypro UK chemical plant formed an enormous vapour cloud that exploded with a force equivalent to 15 tonnes of TNT, destroying the factory and causing widespread damage to the surrounding area. Twenty-eight employees lost their lives. If the accident had taken place on a weekday the toll is likely to have exceeded five hundred. No one who was in Flixborough on that day will ever forget where he or she was and what they were doing at the time the blast occurred.

From Burton upon Stather a steep cliff leads down to the riverside and a cargo wharf. In the Civil War, Colonel St George, Royalist Governor of Gainsborough, built fortifications in the area to protect Gainsborough from attack. Advancing from Hull, Parliamentarian forces under the Earl of Manchester mounted a two-pronged assault by land and along the Trent. Burton Stather and Gainsborough were quickly taken. An outpost of Cavaliers occupying St John's at Alkborough with its vantage point tower were killed and their bodies buried beneath the church floor.

Below Alkborough, the river is a great rolling swell, half a mile wide. Approaching the marshy levels of Blacktoft Sands Nature Reserve, near the end of its epic journey from muddy field on Biddulph Moor, the river narrows to three hundred yards, causing the waters to swirl and boil before merging with the Humber Estuary at Trent Falls.

Nine

Until Tomorrow:
Management, Conservation and the Spirit of the Trent

The course of the River Trent is largely the result of natural forces but nature has been challenged and compromised by man-made interference. The rich resources of the river have been exploited and plundered. Increased use of the waterway as a drain to dispose of waste and effluent from the time of the Industrial Revolution left the upper Trent polluted and sterile for much of its length throughout the 19th and 20th centuries. Pollution of the Trent reached a peak in the 1960s. High levels of toxic organo-phosphate and organo-chlorine pesticides leached into the waterway poisoning the food chain. Power station outfalls pumped out millions of gallons of unnaturally oxygenated warm water daily with disastrous results for wildlife.

Flooding has always been a problem in the Trent Valley. In many places, seasonal inundation has been turned to advantage. Controlled flooding allowed fertile riverborne silts, colloquially known as 'warp', to enrich the soil. Warping drains continued to be widely used into the 19th century. Natural water meadows provided livestock with early grazing. In 1770, floodwaters broke through defences downstream of Dunham causing extensive flooding as far as Littleborough and Marton. Widespread damage to bridges and property occurred in 1795 and 1875. In the wake of industrialisation and rapid population growth in the 19th century vulnerable washlands came under pressure. Natural flood cushions were encroached upon to meet the demand for housing. Ancient Trentside villages

147 *Levels reached by floodwater recorded in the stonework beside Trent Bridge, Nottingham. The scale shows the height in feet above ordnance datum. Normal water level is 68 feet.*

stood behind floodplains that acted as buffers but the lessons of history were forgotten. The Meadows area of Nottingham became densely built-up and suffered the consequences in 1875. Sawley and Long Eaton were swamped in 1932. Hardly anywhere escaped the floods of March 1947. Water levels rose 12 feet above normal at Nottingham's Trent Bridge. Existing defences, many of which were built in the wake of the problems experienced in 1875, proved inadequate. At Morton, floodbanks were breached and countryside as far north as Gunness was inundated.

Major floods, an unpredictable statistical certainty, were infrequent enough to encourage a degree of complacency. Each incident resulted in a knee-jerk flurry of preventative measures. All too often solutions were unimaginative, visually unappealing and in some cases counterproductive. Typical water management schemes involved raising flood barriers, straightening channels and inserting concrete culverts: measures that caused erosion of the riverbanks and in extreme conditions contributed to difficulties by preventing floodwater dispersing. With fragmented responsibilities and without an overarching strategy, local authority activity tended to be piecemeal. After universal problems in 1998 and 2000 and amid increasing concern about the adverse effects of global warming, The Environment Agency issued new guidance for developing flood defences. A River Trent Strategy report was commissioned to identify vulnerable areas and evaluate risk management options taking account of technical, economic, social and environmental considerations. A Catchment Abstraction Management Strategy setting out a licensing strategy for the management of the whole of the River Trent from Biddulph Moor to the Humber Estuary has now been published after a lengthy consultation period. New floodplain maps have

148   *Giant sluices installed in 1952 at Holme Pierrepont significantly reduce the risk of flooding at Nottingham. Five steel gates respond automatically to differing water levels.*

149 *Power stations were built along the Trent corridor to take advantage of the ready water supply. Cottam Power Station is one of the main Trentside generating sites.*

been made available. Nottingham and Burton-on-Trent, the two main urban centres defined as 'High risk', both now have comprehensive flood defences. Modern approaches rely on softer engineering options, working with nature rather than against it. The value of floodplains and washlands in storing excess water has been recognised along with the role played by bankside vegetation and gentle meanders in protecting banks from erosion.

Electricity pylons stalk the River Trent for much of its length. Power stations punctuate the banks. Since the late 1940s, the flared, concave throated symmetry of power station cooling towers has become one of the definitive sights of the Trent corridor. Thirteen stations built

along the river to take advantage of a convenient water supply, extensive rail network, and accessible coalfields, once delivered a quarter of the nation's electricity requirements. The Trent Valley was nicknamed Megawatt Valley. Coal-fired boilers heat water, producing steam to turn a turbine and rotate a generator. Burning coal releases sulphur dioxide, a cause of acid rain, and domestic coal mined in the United Kingdom tends to have high sulphur content.

Age and stricter environmental controls have caught up with the earliest generating centres. Drakelow, once the most powerful generating site in Europe, and High Marnham both closed in 2003. Four of Drakelow's cooling towers were spectacularly blown up in 1998.

Five towers at Meaford, known affectionately to locals as the 'Ugly Sisters', were brought down with explosive charges in 1991. The first of two generating stations at Willington, in business since 1954, closed in 1995 and the second followed in 1999. Rugeley 'A' Station site is now Towers Business Park though the newer 'B' Station alongside is still in action. One of the first modern generating stations to be built was Staythorpe 'A', commissioned in 1946. When Staythorpe 'B' opened in 1962 it was one of the most efficient coal-fired stations in the United Kingdom. Both are now closed and a replacement using gas-turbine technology is planned. A gas-fired station has been built alongside an existing coal-burning plant at Keadby. Ratcliffe-on-Soar, Cottam and West Burton, until the mid-1980s the three largest power stations in the country, are now the main Trentside generating sites. All are fitted with Flue Gas Desulphurisation Units in which gases react with limestone to produce gypsum for use in plasterboard manufacture, a process that removes up to 90 per cent of the sulphur dioxide. Discharges are cooled and oxygen levels balanced before release. Generating companies have been testing renewable bio-mass materials and the idea of co-firing coal with straw is under consideration.

150 *The five-toed feet of otters are webbed and leave distinctive asymmetrical prints up to three inches wide. Front paws are more rounded and slightly shorter.*

Otters were once hunted for their thick, double-layered fur and to prevent them stealing from fisheries. King John established the royal otterhounds and other packs followed. At the turn of the 20th century, 23 packs of otterhounds were registered in the United Kingdom. Most of them were still active in the 1930s but within two decades conservation had become a concern. Otters, a good indicator of the health of a river, disappeared. North American mink, escapees from fur farms first introduced to England in 1929, managed to exploit the niche. Because mink were able to pursue prey into their dens, a water vole population, already under threat from the destruction of breeding sites and loss of bankside vegetation, was decimated. Fish stocks collapsed.

Otters received full legal protection in England and Wales in 1978. Scotland followed suit shortly afterwards. Under the Wildlife and Countryside Act (1981) it is an offence to kill, injure or knowingly disturb an otter or its holt.

In a National Otter Survey carried out between 2000 and 2002, the River Trent and its tributaries showed the biggest increase in otter population in the country. The survey is based on evidence of presence rather than actual sightings. Otters are still scarce and full recovery is far from certain but the results are positive. The return of otters has resulted in a dramatic decline in the number of mink. Otters are bigger, stronger, and well equipped to compete with their rivals. Sightings are rare, partly because otters are alert, shy and most active at night, but they have been reported along the whole length of the river, even in the centre of Stoke-on-Trent. Signs are easier to spot. As well as tracks and runs, look out for droppings or 'spraint'. These are an otter's calling card, left in a prominent position to give others individual information about the animal concerned. Fresh spraint is dark green, often almost black in colour, with a sweet scent of fish and new mown hay. Mink 'scats' are thin with a tapering, twisted end and a strong, unpleasant odour.

151 *Cormorants perching on the buoy-string barrier at Gunthorpe Weir. Historically a coastal seabird in the United Kingdom, their spread inland has been controversial. Many consider the birds greedy predators that damage fish stocks.*

Breeding colonies of cormorants spread along the Trent during the 1980s. Many consider them greedy predators responsible for reducing fish numbers. American red-eared terrapins began to make an occasional appearance when tiny pets bought in the wake of the Ninja Turtles cartoon mania became too big or too much trouble for their bored owners. As the fad waned many were released into waterways. Adults can survive in the wild but cold English conditions prevent successful breeding.

Shoulder-high Himalayan balsam, origi-nally introduced as decorative garden plants by intrepid Victorian plant hunters attracted by their large pink flowers, is rampant along large stretches of the riverbank. A member of the *impatiens* family, the ripe seedcases explode

in the autumn. Seeds are scattered widely and are carried downstream by the river to colonise new areas.

Since 1998, around eighty thousand, two inch long salmon parr reared at Kielder Hatchery in Northumberland have been released into the Trent's River Dove tributary in a joint project managed by the Trent Rivers Trust and Severn Trent Water plc. In October 2001, the first few adults returned, after three years feeding and growing to maturity in the waters around Greenland. Each year, though still small, the number of returning fish grows. For the first time in eight decades, patient observers can hope to witness the muscled silver curve of salmon leaping weirs to reach their spawning grounds.

152 *Introduced by Victorian plant hunters, Himalayan Balsam escaped from gardens and now grows in rampant swathes along much of the Trent. A member of the* impatiens *family with large pink flowers, it has green seedcases that explode when ripe. Seeds are scattered widely and can be carried long distances downstream.*

A cleaner river has improved fish stocks but problems continue. In April 1858, an angler landed a catch of 22 fish weighing 66 lb in just two hours. Not much more than a generation ago, the Trent was the most fished river in England. Before pollution and the rival attraction of well-stocked fishing lakes, crowded banks were common. Now, although average catches show statistical increases, anglers are adamant all is not well. Re-profiling of the river to aid navigation and as part of flood defence measures has speeded up flows and destroyed natural refuges necessary for fish to spawn and where fry can grow. Action is now being taken to recreate suitable sanctuaries. On the Thrumpton Estate an old watercourse is being cleared to create a fish refuge.

More research is necessary before the long-term effects of chemicals released into the river system are fully understood. Fish exhibiting both male and female sexual characteristics have been observed, suggesting that sterility may be a problem. New standards for water to be introduced across the European Union by 2015 will look beyond the narrow measure of water quality and monitor a much wider range of factors across the riparian habitat.

As well as a wealth of resident species, the Trent Valley is an important passage route for birds. Large numbers of migrant waders and wildfowl use the wetland scrapes and nature reserves. Flooded gravel quarries can be too deep and cold to sustain the nutrients necessary to encourage wildlife. By linking them directly to the river, life is breathed into these artificial lakes.

If the River Trent is a priceless asset, it has also been a threat requiring high maintenance to keep under control. In many ways the power-ful river has been tamed, corralled between floodbanks that, in many places, hide it from view. A great artery bled and fed by a series of sluices and drains that control water levels. The mighty aegir rarely roars as once it did, a moving wave up to 10 ft high, audible two miles away and capable of capsizing small boats. But in the right conditions, for example when a prolonged dry spell precedes a high spring tide, it is still an impressive sight. Often it belly dances upstream, a low, breaking ripple of fizzing surf towing the tide.

In recent years, greater awareness of the po-tential for environmental damage and its impact on the quality of life has led to a more sensitive and co-ordinated approach to river manage-ment. Since privatisation in the 1980s, water companies have invested millions of pounds in updating antiquated sewage works. With fund-ing from English Heritage, The Environment Agency and Nottinghamshire County Council, a team from Nottingham and Leeds Universi-ties has produced a detailed three-dimensional model charting the changing topography, land

153   *A low, rippling aegir shimmering in dawn sunlight as it passes between East and West Stockwith.*

154   *Anglers at Colwick Weir around 1900. In the early 20th century the Trent was the most fished river in England.*

use and patterns of settlement in the Trent Valley in Nottinghamshire over ten thousand years. Geological and geographical information is combined to identify potential archaeological hotspots and inform future planning.

The OnTrent initiative is a partnership involving government agencies, local authorities, private industry, landowners and other interested groups in a range of practical projects and policy forums aimed at conserving and enhancing the natural environment and historic heritage of the Trent Valley. Quarry sites along the length of the river are being imaginatively restored as wetland habitats, as a buffer against accidental pollution, and as a leisure resource. At Witches Oak near Shardlow a former quarry has been successfully developed by Severn Trent Water to provide a reserve water supply for the East Midlands, the first time Trent water has been used for a drinking supply since Nottingham's Trent Water Company abandoned their river-fed reservoir in 1845.

Balancing social, economic and environmental needs with custodianship of such a precious resource is a difficult task but the signs are good. Anglers may not yet throng the banks in the same numbers as they once did, but as well as boaters and water sports enthusiasts there are more walkers, joggers, cyclists, and bird watchers than ever, their needs catered for by a range of public, private and voluntary sector partnerships. Waterfront regeneration has been a trigger for wide-ranging redevelopment reconnecting Trentside communities to their river.

Rivers are a potent symbol of renewal and provide an enduring metaphor for the cycle of life. We are born, grow and make our way inexorably to our destiny, our character shaped by events. The Trent too has its own personality, forged over tens of thousands of years. Those of us who love the river share a common bond and yet we are all infused with our own private Trent. It is a seductive spirit.

Sources and Further Reading

Main Sources

British Archaeology, ed. Denison, S. (issue 47, 1999)

Environment Agency Report, *River Trent Strategy: A new way of looking at flooding solutions* (2004)

Harpur-Crewe Papers, Derbyshire Record Office

Humber Archaeology, *Flixborough Anglo-Saxon Settlement, North Lincolnshire* (report, 1992)

Paget MSS, Staffordshire Record Office

Pigot and Co.'s *National Commercial Directory* (1830)

Press Office, Powergen

The Stoke-on-Trent Rivers Strategy (Draft Report), Stoke-on-Trent City Council, Environment Agency, and Severn Trent Water Ltd (2004)

The Proceedings of the Architectural and Archaeological Societies of Lincolnshire and Nottinghamshire (various volumes including):

Cole, R.E.G., *The Royal Burgh of Torksey* (vol. 28, 1905-6)

Transactions of the Thoroton Society (various volumes including):

Braun, H., *Notes on Newark Castle* (vol. 43, 1935)

Griffin, Rev. H.J., *Summer Excursion 1909: Littleborough Church* (vol. 13, 1909)

Holland Walker, J., *An Itinerary of Nottingham* (vol. 29, 1925)

Keats-Rohan, K.S.B., *Prosopon Newsletter* (issue 2, 1995)

Losco-Bradley, P.M. and Salisbury, C.R., *A Medieval Fish Weir at Colwick* (vol. 79, 1979)

Salisbury, C.R., *An Anglo-Saxon Fish Weir at Colwick* (vol. 85, 1981)

Salisbury, C.R., *An Eighth-Century Mercian Bridge over the Trent at Cromwell, Nottinghamshire* (vol. 99, 1995)

Salisbury, C.R., *An Early Tudor Map of the River Trent in Nottinghamshire* (vol. 87, 1983)

Standish, Rev. J., *Attenborough Church* (vol.10, 1906)

Standish, Rev. J., *Margidunum* (vol 12, 1908)

Wood, A.C., *The History of Trade and Transport on the River Trent* (vol. 49, 1950)

Trent & Peak Archaeological Trust (TPA Unit project reports, including):

'Late Neolithic Human Remains from the River Trent in Nottinghamshire' (1996)

Trent Valley GeoArchaeology group (research reports, including):

'Bronze Age Lakes at Aston on Trent' (2002)

University of Leicester Archaeological Services (reports, including):

'Shooting and Fishing the Trent' (1999-2000)

'A Bronze Age Burnt Mound, Willington, Derbyshire' (1999-2000)

    Medieval bridges at Hemington Quarry (project summary 1996)

Willan, T.S., *River Navigation in Northern England* (1975)

William Salt: Collections for a History of Staffordshire (various volumes including):

    Thomas, A.L., *North Staffordshire Transport and Communication in the Eighteenth Century*
        (1934)

Andrews, C.B. (ed.) Byng. J., *The Torrington Diaries* (1935)

Baker, J., 'Buildings on Swarkestone Bridge' (*Derbyshire Miscellany* vol. 13, pt 5, 1994)

Beckett, J.V., *The East Midlands from A.D. 1000* (1988)

Beckwith, I., *The History of Transport and Travel in Gainsborough* (1971)

Beckwith, I., 'Transport in the Lower Trent Valley in the Eighteenth and Nineteenth Centuries'
        (*East Midland Geographer*, vol. 4, pt 2, 1966)

Bede, *The Ecclesiastical History of the English People* (ed. McClure, J. and Collins, R., Oxford
        World Classics, 1994)

Bradshaw, R.P., 'Electricity Production in the Trent Valley' (*East Midland Geographer*, vol. 10,
        pt 1, 1987)

Brown, C., *A History of Newark-on-Trent* (1904)

Deering, C., *An Historical Account of the Ancient and Present State of the Town of Nottingham*
        (1751)

Kingsley, A.G., *The Anglo-Saxon Cemetery at Millgate, Newark-on-Trent, Nottinghamshire*
        (Nottingham Archaeological Monographs, 1989)

Minnitt, B.A., *A Trentside Narrative* (1986)

Owen, C.C., 'The Early History of the Upper Trent Navigation' (*Transport History* vol. 1, 1968)

Polkey, A., *The Civil War in the Trent Valley* (1992)

Rowlands, M.B., *The West Midlands from A.D.1000* (1987)

Stafford, P., *The East Midlands in the Early Middle Ages* (1985)

Secondary Sources and Further Reading

Bennett, F. and Stobbs, G., *Kelham Hall: A Family and a House* (undated)

Bishop, M.W., *The Battle of East Stoke* (1987)

Blackner, J., *History of Nottingham* (1815)

Greenslade, M.W. and Stuart, D.G., *A History of Staffordshire* (1965)

Heath, J., *A Look at Shardlow Past* (1984)

Ingram, J.H., *The River Trent* (1955)

Jervoise, E., *The Ancient Bridges of Mid and Eastern England* (1932)

Kaye, D., *A History of Nottinghamshire* (1987)

Knight, D. and Howard, A. with Elliott, L., Jones, H. and Leary, R., *Trent Valley Landscapes* (2004)

Lord, Peter, *Portrait of the River Trent* (1968)

Marcombe, D. and Borrill, A., *Millgate: a guided walk* (1997)

Morland, W.A., *A Portrait of the Potteries* (1978)

Pask, B.M., *Newark: the Bounty of Beer* (1997)

Smalley, Y. and Tranter, M., *Change in a Derbyshire Village: Weson-on-Trent 1900-1950* (1996)

Stark, A., *History of Gainsborough* (1817)

Wood, A.C., *A History of Nottinghamshire* (1971)

The Bridge: A History of Willington Bridge (1998), research by Gifford, A., Howells, J., Kitching,
        C. and Morrow, E.; compiled by Taylor, J.

Index

Page numbers in **bold** type refer to illustrations.

129